More Praise for
Friends Forever

"With humor, patience, and common sense, Frankel provides adoptive parents with step-by-step guidance for teaching children interpersonal skills that are crucial to making and keeping friends: problem solving, learning how to play fair, making positive choices, and dealing with bullies, meanness, and teasing."
—JoAnne Solchany, PhD, ARNP; *Adoptive Families* magazine

"[Highly] recommended book [for] professionals who work with children and parents, especially child group therapists.... It reinforces our commitment to friendship as a cardinal developmental issue and reminds us that we have a great deal to offer these children and their parents."
—*Journal of Child and Adolescent Group Therapy*

"*Friends Forever* is a book that provides concrete help and supports the lifelong richness that friendships can bring to a child's life. Despite our busy lifestyles, helping children develop authentic friendships is certainly a task worth fostering."
—Sylvia Stultz, PhD, California Society for Clinical Social Work, *Clinical Update*

friends forever

friends forever

*How Parents Can Help Their Kids
Make and Keep Good Friends*

———•———

Fred Frankel, PhD

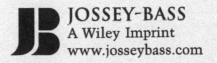

JOSSEY-BASS
A Wiley Imprint
www.josseybass.com

Published by Jossey-Bass
A Wiley Imprint
989 Market Street, San Francisco, CA 94103-1741—www.josseybass.com

Readers should be aware that Internet Web sites offered as citations and/or sources for further information may have changed or disappeared between the time this was written and when it is read.

Limit of Liability/Disclaimer of Warranty: While the publisher and author have used their best efforts in preparing this book, they make no representations or warranties with respect to the accuracy or completeness of the contents of this book and specifically disclaim any implied warranties of merchantability or fitness for a particular purpose. No warranty may be created or extended by sales representatives or written sales materials. The advice and strategies contained herein may not be suitable for your situation. You should consult with a professional where appropriate. Neither the publisher nor author shall be liable for any loss of profit or any other commercial damages, including but not limited to special, incidental, consequential, or other damages.

Jossey-Bass books and products are available through most bookstores. To contact Jossey-Bass directly call our Customer Care Department within the U.S. at 800-956-7739, outside the U.S. at 317-572-3986, or fax 317-572-4002.

Jossey-Bass also publishes its books in a variety of electronic formats. Some content that appears in print may not be available in electronic books.

Library of Congress Cataloging-in-Publication Data

Frankel, Fred D.
  Friends forever : how parents can help their kids make and keep good friends / Fred Frankel.—1st ed.
    p. cm.
  Includes bibliographical references and index.
  ISBN 978-0-470-62450-0 (pbk.)
  1. Friendship in children. 2. Social skills in children. 3. Interpersonal relations.
I. Title.
  HQ784.F7F728 2010
  649'.7–dc22

          2010010012

Printed in the United States of America
FIRST EDITION
PB Printing 10 9 8 7 6 5 4 3 2

CONTENTS

————•————

Acknowledgments   ix

Introduction   xi

PART ONE
How Parents Can Help   1

1 Making Time for Friends   3

2 Curbing Interests That Prevent Friendships   11

3 Developing Interests That Attract Friends   19

4 Using Your Neighborhood School for Friends   27

5 Using Organized Activities to Find Friends   31

6 Improving Your Networking Skills   43

PART TWO
Making Friends   49

7 Joining Others at Play   51

8 Becoming a Good Sport   67

9   Looking for Closer Friends and Joining
    a Friendship Group   79
10 Using the Telephone to Make Friends   87
11 Using Texting and Instant Messaging to
    Connect with Friends   101
12 Having Fun Play Dates   109
13 Becoming a Better Host   125
14 School Break and Vacation Activities That
    Promote Friendships   143

PART THREE

Keeping Friends   151

15 Encouraging Wise Choices   153
16 Discouraging Poor Choices   159
17 Listening to Your Child's Worries   169
18 Having Friends Stolen   175
19 Losing a Close Friend   181
20 Divorce and Moving Away   185

PART FOUR

Dealing with Teasing, Bullying, and Meanness   193

21 Taking the Fun Out of Teasing   195
22 Stopping Rumors   205
23 Staying Away from Children Who Fight   211
24 Dealing with Children Who Bully   217

PART FIVE

Helping Your Child
Out of Trouble   227

25 Working with Adults Who Have Trouble
    with Your Child   229

26 Stopping Your Child's Fighting   239

27 Overcoming Hyperactive Behavior   247

28 Stopping Your Child's Bullying   253

29 Not Noticed by Classmates   259

30 Building Friendship Skills and Overcoming
    a Negative Reputation   267

Notes   269

Resources   281

About the Author   287

Index   289

To Seth Frankel, Rachel Ettner, and Sarah Ettner for showing me the joys and rewards of being a father and helping me learn about children's friendships in a very personal way, and to Susan Ettner for her encouragement and support and showing me what it's like to be part of a loving family

ACKNOWLEDGMENTS

I am thankful for being in the right place at the right time. I am greatly indebted to Bob Myatt, who shared his expertise with me from doctoral work on children's social skills at the University of Mississippi. Through the success of the Children's Friendship program Bob Myatt and I developed at the University of California, Los Angeles, I have met many parents and children. (When their stories have appeared in this book, I have changed names and other identifying details to protect confidentiality.) The help and encouragement of Linda Pillsbury and Cynthia Whitham turned my experiences into this book.

My collaborators on various research projects have also taught me much and helped me to expand the applicability of my approach to children's friendships. Denise Wilfley and her students at the University of California, San Diego, helped apply the techniques, especially those concerned with handling teasing, to children with weight problems. Blair Paley, Mary O'Connor, and her students helped test the techniques with children as young as age six with fetal alcohol spectrum disorders and alcohol-related neurological disorders. Amy Schonfeld and Elizabeth Laugeson introduced and helped test enhancements for cognitively impaired children, teens, and their parents. Erika

Carpenter helped to develop the information on parent networking skills.

I would like to thank all of the people at Jossey-Bass Publishing who made this book a reality: Alan Rinzler, executive editor, for his wise guidance; Nana Twumasi, senior editorial assistant, for launching this book into publication; Carol Hartland, senior production editor, for overseeing production; Bev Miller for her thorough copyediting; and Susan Geraghty for putting the finishing touches on this book. I also would like to thank Jennifer Wenzel, marketing manager, and Erin Beam, publicist, for effectively getting the word out about this book.

INTRODUCTION

———•———

From the Introduction to the Former Edition

When I began my clinical practice in the mid-1980s, a lot of the families coming to me for treatment had children with friendship problems. Conventional treatments (individual, group, and family therapy) were not effective with these problems, and I started to think about what I could do to help. In 1990, my son was five years old and just beginning to make friends by himself. I noticed how he did this and what parents had to do to keep friendships going. I also noticed that other parents in our neighborhood whose children had friends were doing pretty much the same things.

I also looked at what researchers had discovered about children's friendships. The 1980s were productive years for researchers interested in children with friendship problems. Developmental psychologists made breakthroughs. They started by asking children whom they liked and disliked playing with. They found that many children were quietly suffering from friendship problems (10 percent had no friends at all).[1] They then identified the things children did that led to friendship problems and what well-adjusted children did in the same situations.

Some researchers had the patience (and funding) to see what happened to these children as they grew up. What they found was eye-opening: children who had chronic difficulties making and keeping friends were more likely to drop out of school and have drug problems in adolescence.[2] Children who did not have a best friend outside the family (brother and sister don't count here) grew up to be lonely young adults.[3] They found that close friends teach each other social grace and how to solve disagreements.[4] Close friends support each other in stressful times and help each other to look beyond their own needs and become sensitive to others.[5]

Introduction to This Edition

Response to the former edition of this book, titled *Good Friends Are Hard to Find*, has been gratifying. It has been reprinted in five major languages: Arabic, Chinese, Japanese, Korean, and Spanish. It has also been endorsed by government agencies[6] and national public media[7] and received positive reviews from various national interest groups representing therapists,[8] children, and parents.[9]

Several important changes have taken place since the publication of that first edition. Foremost is that parents have become more worried about violence that is spilling out into middle and high schools. The Internet has intruded more into family life through instant messaging (IM) and a flood of information, wanted and unwanted. Video games have become more sophisticated and captivating for children. In response to these pressures, the additional challenges facing parents are considerable, and many of these have trickled down to parents of elementary school-aged children. I have added material to this book to help parents cope with these new challenges.

The field of clinical psychology has also undergone a metamorphosis as a new evidence-based movement in therapy has taken hold. The basic tenet is that treatment programs should be standardized and should be evaluated and modified based on the measured outcome of treatment. The UCLA Children's Friendship Program has been in the forefront of this movement. Over thirteen hundred children and their parents have been helped in our Children's Friendship Training classes (outside of our research studies, we have conducted over 155 of these classes since 1989). An important part of the intervention is homework assignments given to parents and children. These homework assignments form the basis of much of this book. In subsequent sessions, we hear about the experiences of parents and children in following through with these assignments, and we help them adapt the program to their specific situation if necessary. This process has been important in helping me modify and adapt the program, and I have revised this book to incorporate these findings.

The results of clinical trials have been gratifying: improvement on our outcome measures ranged from 70 to 91 percent of children.[10] While we were testing the interaction of our treatment with medication, one possible approach to treating attention-deficit/hyperactivity disorder (ADHD, see Chapter Twenty-Seven), we found that children with ADHD who were taking Ritalin or a similar medication showed improvement at the same level as the children without ADHD.[11] Children with fetal alcohol spectrum disorders improved on all parent and teacher measures when they were prescribed neuroleptic medication, such as risperidone.[12] Children with autism spectrum disorders showed greater improvement when they were not prescribed any medication.[13] Follow-up at sixteen weeks after the end of treatment showed continued improvement.[14] I believe that this is because parents continued to have one-on-one play dates using the techniques they learned from us.

The most important finding has been that one-on-one play dates are the best way to build close friendships.[15] A one-on-one play date happens when your child invites only one guest over and plays with him or her in private. These occasions are the only time when children can get to know each other intimately without interruption, and so they help your child develop and maintain intimate relationships with friends.

How This Book Is Organized

I am adopting some conventions in this book to simplify the presentation. Ninety-five percent of children we have helped were in grades 1 through 6, so examples cover only this age range. Also for ease of reading, I talk about boys and girls in stereotyped interests, for example, boys playing sports and girls playing with dolls. (Tomboys are discussed in Chapter Five in more detail.)

The focus of this book is on helping parents. I have listed citations for those interested in looking at part of the evidence base from many of my summary statements about studies. These are usually journal articles, which were the best or only sources. I have also published a manual of the UCLA program for therapists and readers interested in a more detailed look at how our groups work.[16]

This book is organized into step-by-step plans that address common friendship issues:

1. "The Problem" describes specific problems that the chapter addresses.
2. "Background" helps you to understand causes and solutions of each problem.
3. "Solving the Problem" gives you step-by-step instructions to practice with your child.
4. "The Next Step" tells you which problem to solve next and which chapters to read for relevant information.

You don't need to read this book cover to cover. Just focus on the areas in which your child needs help, solving one problem at a time. I show you the most important rules to teach your child and which problems to solve first. The rules are easy to teach to your child.

I am reminded of the best definition of quality friendship I have come across: "Friendship is a mutual relationship formed with affection and commitment between people who consider themselves equals."[17]

Helping children find and make friends takes a considerable investment. The demands on parents today are enormous. But making time to practice the strategies in this book will help your child to develop quality friendships. The children who improve the most have parents who discuss problems with them and know how to help. You are the best person to help your child solve friendship problems.

friends forever

PART ONE

How Parents Can Help

———•———

Your child needs friends as much as he needs food and exercise. Success in life is influenced by a combination of academic achievement and skill in being friendly towards others.[1] You can help your child find friends.

1

Making Time for Friends

———●———

The Problem

- I'm not sure my child has the time to have friends, what with homework and all of the activities she's in during the school year. What can I do?

Background: Too Busy to Have Friends?

Our lifestyles today leave children less play time than children in the past had, and pull children away from friendships. Teachers depend more on homework (and parents) to teach children, and that added homework spills over into our children's afternoons and evenings. In more families than in the past, both parents work, so families spend less time together during the week. Some use weekends for family time. The bottom line is that there is less time for all of us for friends.

We Misplace Our Time

School-aged children average twenty-seven hours of electronic media viewing per week.[1] And that's just an average—some children watch considerably more. This figure also doesn't include video game play and other computer time. Children are home Saturday morning watching TV, sending instant messages to friends, and playing video games instead of running around and playing with each other. Many parents tell me they are hard-pressed to get everything done, and they are relieved that their children are occupied. But the prevalence of obesity is increasing in children, and the time spent watching electronic media has been targeted as a major contributor.[2] We are sacrificing companionship and health for entertainment.

We Give Away Our Time

Parents tell me they feel they have to put their child in many different structured activities: soccer, scouts, music lessons, computer class, karate. These activities can effectively fill up their child's free time, but they are left with no time for friends.

Children need time for one-on-one play dates—the best way to make friends. Classes and scouts may be productive ways to meet other children, and sports may sometimes be ways to get exercise, but your child needs enough open time for one or two play dates of at least two hours each every week (kindergarten and first graders start out with shorter play dates). You will need to open up more than four hours to make your child accessible to other children's schedules. Even if you and your spouse work, children have all day Saturday and Sunday for play dates.

Solving the Problem: How to Free Up Time for Friends

Freeing up time may involve some simple advanced planning to make adjustments to your weekly schedule. The key is to weigh the longer term importance of each activity and accept that you can engage in the more important activities.

*Step 1: Calculate How Much Time Your Child Has
for Close Friends*

Figure out how much prime time your child currently has for one-on-one play dates. Prime time is when other children are likely to get together with your child. Include only times when

- You are around to supervise.
- Your child can see a single playmate of his choice.
- Your child can play without any siblings around. This may be difficult for you to arrange, but it will be worth the effort.
- Your child and his friend can choose what they want to play.

Table 1.1 shows typical times for play dates, figuring school ends at 2:30.

Don't include sleepover time (Friday and Saturday after 7:00 P.M.) as prime time. Sleepovers are valuable for children who are becoming good friends, but not for the first few play dates with each other.

If both parents work, then play dates from Monday through Friday are not possible, which leaves only seventeen hours of prime time per week. Now figure out how many hours your child has for one-on-one play dates. If your total is less than four hours per week during prime time, go to step 2.

Table 1.1   Prime Times for Play Dates

Days	Prime Times	Total Hours
Monday through Thursday	2:30–6:00 P.M.	14.0
Friday	2:30–7:00 P.M.	4.5
Saturday and Sunday	10:00 A.M.–7:00 P.M.	17.0
Total prime time		35.5

Step 2: Drop Activities That Don't Yield Friendships

Make a list of all the activities your child has during prime time and how many hours each takes up.

The overscheduled child whose weekly activities are shown in Table 1.2 has no time to develop close friendships. He needs to free four hours for this essential activity. What are the things to cut back? Here are my suggestions, set out in the order in which to drop them. Move down the list until you find enough to drop so that your child has those four needed hours.

Activities to Drop

1. TV and video games. These are the least necessary, waste the most time, encourage an unhealthy sedentary lifestyle, and are most easily dropped at the last minute. Schedule a play date to take the place of Saturday morning TV (the TV stays off during the play date).

2. Playing with friends of convenience. These might be a child of your friend, a relative, or a neighbor whom your child does not like. Playing with friends of convenience offers none of the benefits of playing with a close friend. If you can arrange a play date

Table 1.2   An Overscheduled Child

Activity	Weekly Time Commitment
Homework	8 hours
Music lessons and practice	4 hours
Play with neighbor's child I baby-sit	1 hours
Little League games and practice	3.5 hours
Religious school	4 hours
Scouts	1.5 hours
Soccer	3.5 hours
Watching TV, playing video games	9 hours
Origami class	1 hour
Total	35.5 hours

with someone your child likes, cancel these other commitments (a week's notice will be sufficient).

3. Teams or scouts with poor adult supervision benefit no one. Your child is better off at home than being yelled at by a coach or left to his own devices.

4. Teams or scouts outside your neighborhood that don't lead to play dates in your home.

5. Teams that offer your child little opportunity for physical exercise (sitting on the bench, waiting turns). These have few of the health benefits of physical activity and may also encourage a sedentary lifestyle.

6. Nonschool instruction, such as origami, karate, or art class. These activities can be fun and can be a place to meet friends. But there is little benefit in meeting friends if your child never gets to know them.

7. Multiple team or scout activities (Little League, soccer, and swim team practice are too much). Don't cut them all out, just the least productive. All you need is one of these activities at any given time for your child. Your child will benefit little from more than one of these activities at a time if he can't have play dates with friends.

Overscheduled children have more than enough of teams and classes. Each of these activities may have seemed enriching when you signed your child up, but look at the total schedule at this point and set your priorities. Think about eliminating the activity that would lead to the fewest play dates. Open up blocks of time by dropping nonschool classes or activities.

Step 3: Drop Activities That Soak Up Your Time

You can't leave play dates for someone else to supervise. You are the best person to be there to make sure things go well. Your time is valuable and not as productively spent in activities that don't benefit you or your child.

Margaret, for example, is a soft-spoken, pleasant mother of eight-year-old Todd. For the past two years, she has put in many hours as the leader for Todd's Cub Scout den, which has six boys other than Todd. She spends two hours each week planning den meetings, plans and spends the better part of one Saturday each month on a den outing, and spends one hour per month with other den leaders planning Cub Scout pack activities.

In spite of his mother's volunteering twenty-two hours per month for scouts, not one of the other boys has ever invited Todd for play dates. They never invite him to their birthday parties, although they occasionally talk about their parties at Cub Scout meetings in front of Todd. In fact, Todd has no friends at all he can invite to play with.

My heart went out to Margaret when she told me this story. Despite her valiant efforts (Cub Scouts wouldn't exist without parents like Margaret volunteering their time), her child is overlooked by the other children she is helping. Putting this much time into scouts keeps her from helping Todd find children who would be happy to play with him. Here are twenty-two hours each month that she could devote to Todd's benefit. She has three choices at this point:

1. Devote time to arranging play dates with the parents of her Cubs.

2. Look for ways to add Cubs to her den who want to play with Todd.

3. Graciously hand over the den to another parent. She does not owe the others her time. She can tell the other parents she is too busy to continue and they have to find someone else. She can give Todd the choice of continuing with this den, changing to another, or dropping out of scouts.

When I was a Cub master, I saw parents who took choice 3, and no one blamed them; we were glad to have their help while they could give it. The other parents will take over den leadership if they care enough for scouts.

Step 4: Make That Car Pool Work for You and Your Child

Not only do car pools save time, they can also help your child meet children his age who live close by. The common destination gives children something to talk about, and riding in the car (with the radio off) gives them time to talk. Arranging play dates becomes much easier. For example, Darnell's and Clark's moms have car-pooled with each other to get their boys to school. Here's how easily they arrange a play date:

DARNELL'S MOM: Darnell would like to know if Clark can come over to our house this Friday.

CLARK'S MOM: Clark's been asking to play with Darnell, so that I'm sure he'd love it.

DARNELL'S MOM: How about if I just take them over to our house after school when I pick them up?

CLARK'S MOM: That will be great!

Nevertheless, car pools can sometimes work against having friends, as Paul and Joanne found out. They live within two blocks of each other and are good friends. Their sons attend first grade at the same school across town, so they have arranged a car pool there. But Joanne's son behaves poorly at Paula's house, in the car, and at school, and Paula's son does not like to play with this boy. But he does anyway since he doesn't have any other choices.

Although Joanne and Paula are friends, the two boys are not. They are forced to be together in the car and have play dates with each other out of desperation, which is preventing other relationships from sprouting. Perhaps there is a boy in the area whom Paula's son likes and attends the same school. Changing car pools or adding him to the car pool would give Paula's son a more suitable child to play with.

Tips on Forming Car Pools

- Don't make them permanent. Set them up as temporary, so that if you need to change them, no one's feelings will be hurt.

- Set them up so they save you time (but also do your share of the driving).

- Turn a ride home into a play date. Arrange play dates at pickup or drop-off times to save additional time. The other parent can do the same on a day she drives.

The Next Step

You and your child now have more time during the school year to devote to the serious business of making friends (for time management during summer vacation, read Chapter Fourteen). If your child has children to invite over, read Chapters Ten and Twelve before you make your next play date. If your child has difficulty being a good host, read Chapters Twelve and Thirteen before scheduling a play date. If your child spends too much screen time or time playing by himself, read Chapter Two. If your child has trouble meeting new friends, read Chapters Five and Seven. If you could use a few tips on how to connect with other parents to find friends for your child, read Chapter Six.

2

Curbing Interests That Prevent Friendships

———•———

The Problem

- My child frequently prefers playing by herself when her guest is over. What can I do?
- My child likes to watch TV and play video games when his friends come over. Should I allow this?
- Should I worry about my child's obsession with a particular toy?

Background: Interests That Interfere with Friendships

Certain recreational activities, especially TV and video games, can rob your child of friends and interfere with play dates. These activities

- Make it hard to talk to others while they are going on.
- Needlessly steal time away from playing with friends.
- Rob your child of the energy or desire to exercise adequately and play with others.

- Are done just as well, or better, when your child is
  alone.

Too Hooked to Have Friends

Many parents use TV and video games for babysitting while they get other things done. Occasional use of this captivating entertainment is relatively harmless, but some children wind up glued to TV and video games for long periods of time.

Nine-year-old Jeremy spends much of his free time watching TV or playing video games. He doesn't know how to play any board games or the games other boys are playing at recess and shows little interest in sports. Nor does he have any toys at home that are interesting to other children his age. Once Michael, also age nine, came over to his house to play, but they spent the whole time watching TV, barely saying a word to each other. After the play date, Michael told his parents he was bored, and he has since declined invitations to come back to play with Jeremy.

Jeremy's interest in TV has blocked his chances of being friends with Michael. Michael is a people person, the kind of friend who would be valuable for Jeremy to have. The fact that Jeremy would ignore him for two hours is a sad commentary on Jeremy's current priorities. It is difficult to get Jeremy to stop being hooked on TV.

Studies show that children who spend more than two hours each day on average viewing electronic media are at increased risk for overweight and associated physical problems.[1] Children need to learn how to have fun, talk, and solve problems with other children. Watching TV together with others or playing video games for most of a play date prevents this, since the children learn little about each other.

Why is Jeremy so interested in TV to the exclusion of anything else? Is it due to a lack of interactive activities, a bad habit, or an addiction?

Too Much Passion for the Toy, Too Little Regard for the Friend

TV addiction is easy to detect. Another type of addiction that is harmful to friendships is more difficult to spot. It's when children focus on a game or toy, getting overly excited and losing sight of why another child is with them to play.

Natalie is seven years old and an avid collector of dolls. She plays with them by herself for hours at home and in after-school care. When she invites Leah over to play, she insists on playing with her dolls and dictating how Leah should play with them. Leah gets tired of this after forty-five minutes and finds a puzzle to put together. Natalie continues to play by herself, not noticing that Leah is no longer playing with her.

Dolls interest many seven year-old girls, and action figures interest many seven year-old boys. However, Natalie is so interested in playing with dolls that she no longer cares about her friend and what her friend wants to play.

Video games interest many boys. When this is all they want to do with friends, it is interfering with their ability to build deep friendships. You can help the guest and the host by restricting video game play so that they can find out that friendship is more than competition on a video game.

If your child has too much passion for one toy, it's time to act.

Solving the Problem: Curb Addictive and Exclusive Interests

Parents can weed out interests that are destructive to friendships and nurture interests that build friendships. Nurturing friendship-building interests is presented in the next chapter. First, curb TV and video game addiction and interests that exclude other children.

Step 1: Remove Temptation and Easy Access to Electronic Media

Move the TV and video games from your child's bedroom to public areas so that you can easily see when they are being overused. Removing TV from eating areas and turning the TV off during meals gives your child the message that media viewing is not something to be done at every available moment and that TV and eating don't necessarily go together.

Let's say that Mom sees Carl taking his dinner plate to the family room, where the TV is located:

MOM: I would like us to eat dinner together as a family. I want to hear about your day and not have to talk over the TV.

CARL: But I really wanted to watch this program.

MOM: Talking to your family is more important than watching TV.

PLAN A

Carl brings his dinner plate back to the table, and Mom thanks him.

PLAN B

If Carl doesn't come to the table, Mom warns Carl that if he doesn't come to the dinner table, he will lose TV for the evening. If Carl still doesn't come to the table, then the TV privileges are lost for the evening.

Step 2: Set and Enforce a Reasonable Weekly Schedule

A modest amount of TV and video game play at the right time is acceptable. At the beginning of each week, select a reasonable menu of TV fare from the weekly TV listings together with your child (ideally no more than ten total hours of TV and video games for the week, with less being better). Circle the programs you select, so you and your child know what to do when your child wants to watch a TV program: if it isn't circled, it isn't watched.

(Your child doesn't have to watch a program just because it's circled.) Schedule video games for only certain hours.

Dad hears the TV in the adjacent room on and finds that his son James is watching it. Dad checks the TV listings kept next to the TV and finds the program James is watching isn't circled.

DAD: Is that one of the programs we agreed you could watch?

JAMES: I think so.

DAD: Take a look at the listing.

JAMES: [Sees it is not circled] Well, I'm bored, and I have nothing to do.

DAD: At 6:00 we have circled your Nickelodeon program. What can you do until then?

JAMES: I guess I can play with my blocks.

DAD: That's a good idea. Want me to help you get them out?

If James doesn't comply, then Dad warns him that he will lose his TV privileges for the evening. If James still doesn't comply, he immediately loses his TV privileges for the evening.

Step 3: Make a Deal

In step 2 you learned how to set your child's maximum number of hours of leisure time devoted to TV and video games. Elementary school children have more important things they have to do, like homework, which takes priority. Make a deal with your child to do what you want first, and then what he wants—for example:

DAD: Do your homework for thirty minutes, and then you can take a ten-minute break to play a video game.

The rule here is, "First you work, then you play." Allow your child to play video games only after he first completes something necessary. Your child is more likely to do the important things, and he will reduce video game and TV time. This also works well for the addictive interest:

MOM: Natalie, you need to find another toy to play with for thirty minutes before you play with your dolls.

NATALIE: But I don't like to play with anything else.

MOM: You need to give your dolls a rest and give another toy a try. What's it going to be? Roller blades? Painting?

NATALIE: I'll roller-blade, then.

MOM: Good. Roller-blade for the next thirty minutes, and then you can play with dolls.

If Natalie refuses to give up her dolls for thirty minutes, then she is warned that she will lose the dolls for the evening.

It is now up to Mom to enforce this as a minimum time for roller-blading: Natalie can't play with dolls for the next thirty minutes. Mom does not have to remind Natalie if she roller-blades for longer than thirty minutes unless Natalie asks to be reminded. If Natalie stops roller-blading before thirty minutes, tell her to continue with roller blades or find something else.

Step 4: Don't Let an Interest Exclude Playmates

If your child has an interest that sometimes excludes guests when they come over to play, make a deal with your child right before the playmate comes over:

DAD: When Michael comes over, it's time to play with him, so no TV. Have Michael help you pick a game to play.

JEREMY: What if Michael wants to watch TV?

DAD: If he asks, just tell him your parents don't allow TV when guests are over.

Natalie's mother makes a pact with her:

MOM: [Fifteen minutes before Leah comes over] You can play with dolls if you agree to let Leah be in charge of what you play. You have a choice: either let Leah be in charge of what you play, or we'll put the dolls away until Leah leaves. What would you like to do?

NATALIE: I'll let Leah pick what we do.

MOM: Good. We'll give it a try. If you can't let Leah choose, then you'll have to put the dolls away. Okay?

NATALIE: Okay.

PLAN A

If Natalie insists on continuing to play with dolls when Leah is no longer interested, Mom takes her dolls away for the remainder of the play date. She also makes dolls off-limits for the next few play dates. This is how she makes the point that friends are more important than dolls. Natalie is not allowed to bring dolls to school or after-school care, since it is likely she is behaving the same way there.

PLAN B

If Natalie lets Leah choose, this alternative is helping Natalie kick her addiction. Mom makes the same pact each time another girl comes over to play.

The Next Step

Congratulations! You have helped your child cut down on activities that cut out friends. Now it's time to find activities that require playmates. In the next chapter, you will learn how to help your child develop interests that attract friends.

3

Developing Interests That Attract Friends

———•———

The Problem

- My daughter doesn't have the same interests as other girls. What should I do?
- My child doesn't seem to want to play with other children. What can I do about this?
- My child isn't a sports person. What should I do about it?

Background: Cultivation of a Child's Interests

Mutual interests are the basis of friendship. I have several acquaintances whom I like very much, but when I think about getting together with them, I can't think of anything to do that we would both enjoy. That's why they're only acquaintances.

Solitary interests such as reading help make a well-rounded human being, but they don't help children find friends. This chapter shows you how to nurture interactive interests that attract friends. These are activity interests like board games, sports, doll play, and pretend games, which feed friendships. Children with friends have interests that make them want to play and talk with others.

The playground doesn't supply toys, so eight-year-old Roberto took a spongy football from home when he went to the playground. None of the other boys there had thought to bring a toy, and within a matter of minutes, and without asking anyone to play, Roberto immediately had two playmates. He isn't that skilled at football, just skilled enough so that he can enjoy a game of catch. The three boys tossed the ball around for an hour before they got tired.

As with all other icebreakers, it's not enough for Roberto to have the toy. He must know how to use it, or the children will not like playing with him. The spongy football helps the boys get to know each other because the toy is easy to share. If the toy were a radio-controlled car, other children would be attracted. But instead of harmonious play for an hour, you'd see minor squabbling for fifteen minutes over whose turn it is.

Hannah began attending a dance class with two other nine-year-old girls she knew, and she met another girl in the class who also went to her school. After a few months, the four girls started doing things together. They talk about this class endlessly, practice new routines together, and trade clothes.

Studies show that girls include others in their friendship group slowly.[1] It takes a while for Hannah and her friends to form a friendship group: they meet regularly at class, and the common activity leads to common interests, which gives them something to talk about and a reason to get together.

You can help your child become interested in activities that attract others. If you've tried and your child resists learning new games, you can overcome this.

Solving the Problem: Increase Your Child's Interest in Interactive Toys

Some toys draw your child to play with others. But your child won't know how much fun they are until he starts to play with them.

Step 1: Help Your Child Select Useful Interactive Toys

Useful interactive toys are fun to play with only if they are played with someone else. Make sure your child has some interactive toys.

Jason is seven years old and has never gone over to another child's house or invited another child over to his house. He has plenty of books, he likes to draw and has art materials, and he has lots of videotapes. But he doesn't know how to play games that other children his age play. For example, while his classmates are playing handball at recess, Jason is digging in the sandbox by himself.

If you have asked your child what toys he wants or taken him to toy stores and he doesn't want anything, you may think he lacks interest in toys. But your child may not be able to make an informed choice. In Jason's case, his parents can generate the interest. They start by getting one inside and one outside toy that has these important qualities:

- *Requires two persons (indoor toys) or at least two persons (outdoor toys) to play.* If your child likes to play with these, he will be hungry for playmates.

- *Does not encourage aggression.* Water pistols seem harmless, but feelings can get hurt when kids get soaked. Avoid toys with projectiles of any kind— arrows or ninja weapons.

- *Is fun for you and your child to play.* You will teach him the game, so you might as well enjoy it.

- *Has simple rules.* Your child will not need your help to play with a friend, your child won't lose patience learning the game, and you won't lose patience teaching it. Your child can easily teach it to others who don't know how to play.

- *Does not take too long for your child to play.* If he loses interest in games after an hour, get a game that usually ends within forty-five minutes.

- *Is inexpensive.* It will not be a great loss if it isn't
  played or if pieces are lost or damaged.

Balls and jump ropes are useful outdoor toys. Four square, light
plastic balls, and spongy balls are excellent because they are easy
to hit and catch, but can't be easily hit out of the play yard.
Chinese and regular jump ropes and hopscotch are portable. To
get more ideas, watch (with your child) what other children are
playing at school or a local playground.

Board games are useful activities for your home. Starting in
second grade, my son and his friends were able to play Parcheesi,
checkers, Don't Break the Ice, Mr. Wiggly, and Chutes and Ladders
without adult help. They needed adult help with Clue Junior and
Monopoly Junior until fourth grade and could play Monopoly by
fifth grade (but make sure there is enough time to set up and play
the whole game). Use the recommended ages on the game as
a guide.

Discourage any game that your child is too hooked on so that
she no longer cares if she is playing with someone else. Discourage
games that involve trades, because someone's feelings may be hurt
by an unfair trade. Avoid focusing on games that require specialized knowledge that very few other children have (Dungeons &
Dragons, Magic Cards, chess, or Mastermind, unless you know his
friends like to play them too).

Step 2: Play with Your Child

Children have to watch a game played or try to play it themselves in order to become interested. Play with your child to get
him interested in these toys. Start with a game that you like to
play, so that you will have fun too. I find this is an especially
important activity for dads who are, want to be, or need to be
kids at heart. Studies show that the self-esteem of boys and girls
is higher when their dads play with them regularly[2] and enjoy
the games they play.[3]

Seven-year-old Mary doesn't know the rules to any board games or sports. When she plays with other girls, she has difficulty keeping up, since the rules are new to her. She frequently annoys the others by making up her own rules without their agreement, and then she argues over who is correct instead of having fun.

Mary's dad starts with a game with a few simple rules and avoids playing games where she makes up the rules. Either of two things will happen next:

- Mary obeys the rules of the simpler game. She probably made up her own rules to the other games because she was embarrassed that she didn't know them. Mary's dad teaches her the rules of more games and goes slowly.

- Mary continues to make up rules. She wants to be in charge, but her dad doesn't let her make up rules as she goes along. He discourages this behavior:

MARY: I get to go twice.

DAD: [In a quiet, neutral tone of voice] It's no fun for someone else to play unless you stick by the rules.

MARY: But I want to go twice.

DAD: We'll have to stop. I'll be glad to play with you some more when you obey the rules.

MARY: Okay, you go next.

DAD: Thank you [then slightly exaggerates that he is enjoying the game].

Allow your child to negotiate rules. Negotiation means that the child gets others to agree before going on—for example, Mary asks rather than insists she go again. Other kids can say no to this but most won't, so Dad allows this:

MARY: [Throws the basketball and misses] I wasn't ready. Can I go again?

DAD: Okay.

Another possibility is to agree on the rules before the start of play:

MARY: Let's have chanceys [that is, going again if you miss]. Okay?

DAD: I tell you what. You can have chanceys and I won't. Okay?

MARY: Okay.

Step 3: Make Sure Your Child Wins at First

One reason that some children don't like interactive toys is that they get discouraged at first when they lose. So when you are start-ing to play what is a new game for your child, you can rig it so that your child experiences winning during the time he ordinarily would be discouraged. Some people call this reverse cheating. I call it encouragement. Be subtle about it, so your child won't notice you're doing this. The goal is to encourage your child to feel con-fident and like the game so that she will want to play it. You continue to let her win until she becomes confident in her abilities, and by then she's hooked on the game. But then you'll be sunk because she will get tired of playing with you and move on to others her age who are closer in skill. Wallow in your success! Don't worry. She'll come back to you to teach her some more games.

Step 4: Use Tactful Praise with Your Child

Tactful praise is the most powerful way you can improve your child's self-confidence. School-aged children are very sensitive and feel put down if praise isn't tactful. Here's how to tactfully praise kids between five and twelve years old:

- *Eye contact:* Look your child in the eye.
- *Body language:* Make sure you are as close to your child as the situation will allow. Calling out a praising remark from the sidelines near your child is more effective than

from the other side of the field. Leaning over toward your child during a board game is better than yelling.

- *Voice tone:* Have your voice be clearly audible and slightly warm (for children above seven) or very warm (for five to seven year olds). Be louder from the sidelines. Too much warmth makes older children feel you're treating them like a baby.

- *Content:* Make it short, but say exactly what your child did that you liked:

    "It was nice of you to let me go first."

    "That was a nice try."

    "Good move."

- *Timing:* Praise is private, not distracting, and given as soon after the act as possible. Don't wait for the perfect behavior to praise. Start with 25 percent of perfect. The better times to praise are
    - Right after a clever or considerate move in a board game.
    - Immediately after a good catch in a baseball game.
    - On the way home from a team practice or class.

- *Avoid discouraging statements:*
    - Don't talk about your child's faults or what she can't do well in front of others.
    - Don't label your child in a negative way: "He's not a sports person."
    - Don't label your child by comparison: "He's more athletic than his brother."
    - Don't spoil praise, for example: "That's good! Now why couldn't you have done that before?" or "Next time I'm sure you'll do better." These are demoralizing statements.

You may see your child glow after tactful praise. Some children do, and others don't, but they are usually more willing to play with you the next time you ask. They may even ask you to play.

Use lots of tactful praise with your child for two reasons: it makes your child feel better about her own performance, and it's catching. When you praise your child for trying ("nice shot," "good try"), she will begin to use it with other children. Other children prefer to play with a child who praises rather than criticizes them.

The Next Step

If you've followed the steps in this chapter, you've helped your child become a better playmate and raised your child's self-confidence. You've expanded your child's interest in activities that will be fun for her to share. Once she has a couple of dependable activities, the children she plays with will expand her interests more. The next chapter helps you to help your child meet others who will want to be better friends.

4

Using Your Neighborhood School for Friends

————————●————————

The Problem

- My child is not meeting any children he likes. How can I help?

- I don't see any children out in my neighborhood, but I know there are some. How can I help my child find them?

Background: The Social Advantages of a Neighborhood School

Children are invisible in many neighborhoods (they usually are indoors or in their backyard). They become more visible at the neighborhood school.[1] If your child attends a neighborhood school (one that is within a ten-minute drive from your home), you can use the following social advantages:

- Your child can meet children at school who live nearby and thus are accessible for after-school social contacts. It will be easier for you to hang around at school and meet other parents, which is one of the most productive ways of helping your child find friends (read Chapter Six if this does not come easily to you).

• Children don't have far to go for play dates. And when they get older, they can plan their own play dates better since transportation is less of a problem.

Nine-year-olds Jayden and Angel have become best of friends. They have attended the same school together since kindergarten and been in the same classrooms for two years. Their parents can easily arrange play dates, since they frequently meet on the school grounds and talk to each other. Both boys live within walking distance of the school and each other. They frequently call each other to find out about homework. Both mothers are in the school PTA and frequently work together on school fundraisers.

One parent who lived outside a small town told me that she followed the school bus home one day to see who lived at the stops before and after her home. She then asked her child if she liked to play with the children getting off at those stops. When her child said she did, she had her child get their phone numbers.

If your child goes to your neighborhood school and has trouble finding playmates, adults at the school may provide valuable help in identifying potential friends.

Solving the Problem: Using your Neighborhood School to Find Friends

Teachers will often know your child well enough to suggest others who would make good playmates. These potential playmates may wind up being good company during recess and lunch. The daily contact is likely to lead to deeper friendships.

Step 1: Contact Your Child's Teacher

Ask the teacher (or an after-school care supervisor or previous teacher who had a good relationship with your child) if it's a good time to talk privately for a few minutes or plan a meeting for the near future. Tell her you're hoping to expand your child's sources for potential playmates. Then ask if he or she can suggest a classmate. Ask her reasons for the choice. Consider whether the reasons are good.

Good Reasons to Pick a Classmate

- The child's behavior is acceptable.
- Your child and the other child have common play interests.
- The two children sometimes play or work in class together and seem to get along well and like each other. If the teacher does not know this, ask if he or she will observe them in the next couple of weeks.
- The parents of this child may be receptive to having play dates with your child.

Poor Reasons to Pick a Classmate

- Both children have attention-deficit/hyperactivity disorder.
- One child needs the help the other child can provide. For instance, your child can tutor him in math or help him control his behavior. This doesn't lead to a friendship between equals.

Step 2: Contact the Parents of the Child Your Teacher Suggests

If the parents pick up or drop off their child at school regularly, use the steps in Chapter Six for networking with other parents if you need them.

If the parents are hard to meet, it sometimes works to give the teacher a note from you to send home with the child or e-mail the parents. Here's a sample note:

Dear JJ's parents,

Our boys are in Mrs. [teacher's name] third-grade class together. My son talks a lot about your son. They are both interested in [teacher's identified common interest]. If it would work for your family, perhaps we could get the boys together after school or on the weekend some time. Please give a call if you are not too busy. Thanks!

Sign your name and leave contact phone numbers, and enclose a picture of your child with the note in case the child doesn't know your child's name. Then let the other parents make the next move.

The Next Step

You've now found potential friends through your neighborhood school. Convenience is only one of many advantages of these resources. You and your child can make easily maintained and enduring friendships. If you need more neighborhood resources, Chapter Five may help. However, if your child has a negative reputation at his school, read the chapters in Part Two next.

5

Using Organized Activities to Find Friends

———●———

The Problem

- How can I help my child find friends through organized activities?
- My child's friends live too far away to have play dates. What can I do?
- My daughter is a tomboy. How can I help her find friends?

Background: Organized Activities and Your Child's Friendships

The most common suggestion parents give each other to help their child make friends is to put them in an organized activity—usually a team, class, or scouts. This is a helpful suggestion because children are likely to find others with common interests, but it's only the first step. Research shows that organized activities by themselves don't improve friendships.[1] But by taking the steps in this chapter you can ensure that friendships develop outside the activity.

Gender Issues and Friendships

Studies show that activities for "girls only" enhance a girl's self-esteem better than coed activities do.[2] Although having friends of both genders is desirable, it is important to encourage same-sex friendships, since children generally segregate themselves by gender in the school yard.[3] A boy will be lonelier without a same-sex friend to hang around with at recess.

Girls with play interests more usually played by boys (tomboys) can have a more difficult social experience. Boys will accept tomboys on the school playground if they are competent in sports. However, tomboys may be considered second-class citizens, and many boys are less likely to admit they are close friends with a girl. It may be difficult to make play dates for tomboys with a boy, especially if the boy is from a more traditional family. This may be due to misconceptions about the origins and life course of tomboys. Tomboy behavior typically starts at age five and ends by age thirteen without any other established consequences.[4] Surveys of the girls[5] and their parents[6] indicate that about 50 to 63 percent of elementary and middle school girls consider themselves tomboys. With such a high prevalence of girls who at least consider themselves to be tomboys, it seems worthwhile to encourage these girls to have friendships with both boys and girls, especially with other tomboys. A good place to start looking is in sports activities for girls.

Mirella has always preferred wearing boys' clothes, loves to play all sports, and is exceptionally coordinated. When she was five, she played only with the boys in her group day care because the small group of girls had strong preferences for playing with dolls, doing arts and crafts, and dressing up in feminine clothes. When she entered kindergarten, she quickly established friendships with both boys and girls who didn't mind playing tag. Some of the girls on her soccer team initially joked about her clothes, until their parents and they saw that she was largely responsible for their team scoring goals.

Finding Organized Activities in Your Neighborhood

Your neighborhood usually extends to within a ten-minute drive of your home. Whether or not your child attends a school in your neighborhood, it's important for you to use your neighborhood resources to find children with whom your child can easily play. You might even find a parent you want to be friends with.

There are three varieties of neighborhood activities to consider: classes (dance, ballet, karate, science), groups (scouts, theater, day camps), and team sports. They share the following possible benefits:

- They offer opportunities to meet other children and parents.
- They provide a place to see others frequently.
- They provide topics of conversation and shared interests.

Team sports may provide the following additional benefits for your child:

- Promoting physical exercise for better health
- Learning how to work in a group
- Learning how to lose gracefully

Never involve your child in more than two activities at a time, because you won't have enough time for one-on-one play dates. You say you don't know of any neighborhood resources? Take a driving tour of your neighborhood with your child after school one day or on the weekend:

- Look for local parks that are safe and adequately maintained where children your child's age are playing. Go into the park office, and check for after-school programs, team sports, and vacation day camps. Many of these are seasonal, with teams corresponding to their season of professional play. Sign-up is usually one to two months before the start of the season.

- Look for public and private schools. Your neighborhood school yard may have after-school play programs open to your child even if he doesn't attend that school.

- Call the scouting district office. They will put you in touch with leaders of units in your area. Scouts reorganize every September. If you call then, you stand a better chance of getting your child into newly forming groups. Later in the year, it is relatively rare that accommodations can be made.

Solving the Problem: Joining Neighborhood Organized Activities

Once you've found an activity that looks good to you and your child, take the steps that follow.

Step 1: Have Your Child Give the Activity a Try

Your first priority is to get your child to give the activity a try. Make it mandatory that she go at least twice so that she can make an informed choice. Nine-year-old Margarita resists new activities but has some athletic ability:

> MOM: How about taking gymnastics?
> MARGARITA: No. It's boring, and I won't know anyone there.
> MOM: Have you ever seen the class?
> MARGARITA: No, but I don't think I'd like it.
> MOM: There's a class this Saturday. I want you to try it for at least two times.
> MARGARITA: Do I have to?

MOM: Yes. If you don't like it after the second time, then we can stop if you want.

If you can't get your child to try new activities, read Chapter Twenty-Nine.

Step 2: The First Time in Any Activity, Make Sure Your Child Follows Four Basic Rules

It's important for your child to make a good first impression. He will not make friends if he doesn't follow these basic rules of etiquette:

1. Take the activity seriously; don't clown around.
    Children should be quiet and attentive to the adult
    instructor. Making faces or silly sounds or whispering is
    annoying to everyone.

2. Don't try to make friends or talk to other children while
    you're supposed to be paying attention to the adult. This
    is also annoying to everybody.

3. Stay in your own assigned area; don't interfere with
    someone else's performance. Telling other children what
    to do or running all over the field to make catches are
    clear violations of this rule.

4. Don't criticize others. Either praise others or be quiet.

Ask yourself if your child can follow these four basic rules. If the answer is yes, go on to step 3. If not, review these four rules with your child immediately before you try out the new activity:

DAD: I'm glad you're going to give Little League a try. I think you'll have fun. I want you to show everyone how nice you are. I want you to notice how the other kids are taking Little League seriously and that no one is clowning around. The coach will tell you where to play, and that's where you have to stay.

ANDREW: I know that.

DAD: Good. If anyone doesn't listen to the coach and plays in your position, tell me after practice, okay?

ANDREW: Okay.

DAD: If you see someone you want to make friends with, let's try to talk to him after practice, or maybe before the next practice, okay?

ANDREW: Okay.

Notice how Dad left out rule 4 (Don't criticize). There's no helpful way to introduce this rule to your child before it happens. It works better to look for times when he breaks this rule and tell him about it then. Supervise from the sidelines if you're not sure of your child.

PLAN A

If your child follows these rules, praise him child on the way home (see tactful praise in Chapter Three). Then move on to step 3.

PLAN B

If your child violates one or more of the four basic rules, pull him aside immediately after the rule breaking and quietly tell him the rule. Secure a promise from him to obey it:

DAD: [Observes Andrew getting into an argument with another boy and immediately walks over] Andrew, I need to speak to you for a moment. Come here, please.

ANDREW: [Keeps arguing]

DAD: [Getting between Andrew and the other child] I need to speak to you. Come with me. [Takes Andrew off to the side] You need to be quiet and watch home plate while you're in the outfield.

ANDREW: But he was bothering me.

DAD: Then you need to stand far enough away from him so he won't bother you. Can you do that?

ANDREW: Okay.

DAD: Thanks.

If Andrew obeys his dad, then he can continue with practice. Dad uses tactful praise with Andrew after practice and continues to supervise Andrew until he is sure his son follows the four basic rules.

PLAN C

If your child continues to break the four basic rules, it's time to pull your child out of this activity. It doesn't benefit Andrew to continue with this activity if he can't behave appropriately. Andrew's dad needs to help him learn the rules of a good sport (these are set out in Chapter Eight). In the meantime Andrew should avoid the following types of activities:

- Activities that involve a lot of waiting such as baseball.

- Competitive activities, which bring out the worst in some children.

- Combative activities such as karate, which are difficult for children who have trouble confining kicking and hitting to practice.

Step 3: Evaluate the Adult Supervisor

Your next priority is to ensure that your child will have a satisfactory experience that will build self-confidence rather than damage it. The benefits your child gets from sports and classes will depend on the adult supervisors. Most sports programs and public parks depend on volunteer coaches (although professionals generally run martial arts classes for kids). Some of these coaches are looking to make a name for their school, and they put the welfare of the children second. Here are qualities of both good and poor supervisors:

Good Supervisor	Poor Supervisor
Tries to teach children elements of playing or performing without overly high expectations	Kids doing their best isn't good enough; demands perfection
Praises children for personal best or trying	Yells at children for not doing better
Gracefully accepts the game official's rulings	Argues with the game officials
Works children at practice with a plan for improvement	Has no plan; holds poorly thought-out practices with little or no instruction
Lets all of the children have fun	Plays favorites while others warm the benches and receive no instruction
Teaches consideration for others and graceful winning and losing	Teaches physical roughness to win; boasts for winning, argues for losing

You won't find a perfect adult supervisor, although I do give most coaches and teachers high marks and have rarely seen a poor coach working with first through third graders. In contrast, many coaches who work with children ages ten and older focus on winning and overlook sportsmanship to varying degrees. I understand their focus on winning: older children begin to see the team as a job in which others are counting on them. They are demoralized when they play on a team with kids who can't play as well as everyone else. But this doesn't justify poor sportsmanship.

Officials can help parents and coaches know when to draw the line. They need to eject adults (more often parents than coaches in my experience) who are verbally or physically abusive to others.

If your child is on a team with a coach who shows many of the qualities of a poor supervisor, you have two alternatives:

1. Switch your child to another team. This will be hard to do, but it's always worth a try.

2. Withdraw your child from the team. You probably don't want to invest your precious time in an activity that will frustrate you and your child. This way you can avoid a demoralizing experience.

Step 4: Cautiously Involve Yourself in the Activity

Next, get to know other parents while your child is getting to know the other children. Hang out where the other parents are and socialize with them (see Chapter Six if this is not easy for you). Join other parents as they watch the activity. If several parents are helping as assistants, offering to help may be an opportunity to get to know them. However, if your child has social problems, try not to be a coach-parent, which has these drawbacks:

-   If you're like most other parents, the competition will get some juices flowing in you, and you will not be available to promote your child's social growth.

-   Coaches may be more negative with their own child than with others on the team.

-   Other children on the team (or their parents) may think your child is getting preferential treatment and resent this.

-   The child of the coach may misbehave more than the other kids.

Step 5: Make Play Dates with Children Your Child Likes

This is the step that gives your child the more lasting social benefits of your work. You've met other parents, and your child has met other children, and your child has made a good first impression. Now you can make arrangements to get the children together. Start this process by asking your child in private if there is anyone he would like to play with:

DAD: Is there anyone on your Little League team you would like to invite over for a couple of hours?

ANDREW: I don't know.

DAD: How about Tommy? You seem to get along with him, and I can ask his dad.

ANDREW: Okay.

Start with a short play date before or after practice. See Chapters Ten and Twelve for how to do this.

• • •

I have summarized these steps for joining activities.

✓ Checklist for Joining Neighborhood Organized Activities ✓

Step 1: Make the first two visits mandatory; then let your child choose if she wants to continue.

Step 2: The first time in any activity, make sure your child follows four basic rules. It's important for your child to make a good first impression. He will not make friends if he doesn't follow these basic rules of etiquette:

1. Take the activity seriously; don't clown around. Children should be quiet and attentive to the adult instructor. Making faces or silly sounds or whispering is annoying to everyone.

2. Don't try to make friends or talk to other children while you're supposed to be paying attention to the adult. This is also annoying to everybody.

3. Stay in your own assigned area; don't interfere with someone else's performance. Telling other children what to do or running all over the field to make catches are clear violations of this rule.

4. Don't criticize others. Either praise others or be quiet.

   Plan A: If your child follows these rules, praise your child on the way home (see tactful praise in Chapter Three). Go on to step 3.

   Plan B: If your child violates one of the basic rules, pull him aside and quietly tell him the rule. Secure a promise from him to obey. If he obeys, use tactful praise.

   Plan C: If your child continues to break the four basic rules, pull him out of this activity, and teach him the rules of a good sport (Chapter Eight).

Step 3: Evaluate the adult supervisor. If you have a poor supervisor, switch your child to another team or discontinue the activity; otherwise go on to step 4.

Step 4: Cautiously involve yourself in the activity, get to know other parents, and avoid being a coach-parent.

Step 5: Make play dates with children your child likes. (See Chapter Six for this.)

The Next Step

You and your child have taken best advantage of that organized activity. Your child doesn't have to be talented in an activity to use it to meet friends; he needs only to know enough about it to have fun and choose others to play with who are at the same skill level. You have used that activity to help your child meet friends and help you network with other parents. If you need suggestions on how to improve your networking ability, read the next chapter. Many children can take it from here, but some will need to learn how to make friends on their own. Chapter Seven looks at how to help your child with this skill.

6

Improving Your
Networking Skills

———————●———————

The Problem

- I don't find it easy to talk to people I don't know. How can I network with other parents and help my child find friends?

Background: Joining a New Community

Being a parent will naturally change your social networks. You become more interested in talking about children and learning from others about how to make parenting easier and more fun. I remember how awkward I felt when I first started to network. But like any other skill that can be learned, it got easier with practice, and I made a good friend in the process.

Social Support for You and Your Child

Sandy is a kind, forty-two-year-old single woman who adopted seven-year-old Barbara two years ago. Although both had some rocky times adjusting to each other, they get along quite well now. Sandy belongs to a socially active church and is friends with many of the single adults and couples without children in the congregation. But she knows no other parents of seven-year-old girls. She drops her daughter off at Brownie meetings, but doesn't have time to talk to the other parents. Although her daughter is well behaved and liked by other children at school, she has no close friends and is often lonely for a playmate.

Barbara changed Sandy's life in many important ways, but Sandy's social supports failed to support Barbara's needs. I recommended to her that she meet the parents of girls in Barbara's class. As Sandy began to meet these parents, she arranged play dates, and Barbara began to develop closer friends.

There are two different categories of social support:

> *Emotional support:* Some adults talk with you about things that are bothering you or themselves. You turn to them, and they to you, about life decisions and conflicts with other adults. These are your closest friends and family.
>
> *Helpful support:* Parents you share car pools or trade babysitting with are examples.

When you think about your helpful support, notice that the people close by, in your neighborhood or at work, help you more often because they are more accessible.

Many parents are aware that the African proverb that "it takes a whole village to raise a child" means that they would be lost without the help of their neighbors and local resources in providing their children with many quality life experiences. They join a new community of parents when they have children. Some find it easier to join than others. Here are some techniques that more successful parents use.

Times and Places to Network

If you followed the advice in Chapters Four and Five, you have the names of potential playmates for your child. There are certain times and places better suited for networking. Sometimes you see other parents lingering to network with others. I've noticed that most lingerers are moms. Moms of many first graders linger, but by about fourth grade, only a couple of moms are lingering. If you're not a working parent, try both before- and after-school or neighborhood activities to see when most of the other parents are present. If you're a working mom, you might try to do it in the morning, before school starts or be sure to participate in your school's "Bingo night" or other activities. It takes a few minutes of your time to exchange hellos and get to know other parents who are also lingering so that they know you when you ask for play dates for your child. Here is a list of possible places to linger:

- Pickup or drop-off time at school or classes when parents are waiting for their child to start or finish an activity. If your child takes a bus to school then the bus stop might be a good place to linger.
- Parent meetings for school or other activities.
- While volunteering at fundraisers or scouts.
- Religious services or activities.
- Watching sports games and practices.
- The neighborhood park.

Solving the Problem: Steps to More Effective Networking

Step 1: Identify Which Parents You Want to Meet

When you pick up your child at the end of the activity, look for other kids who are with your child or are walking out with your child. Ask your child (in private) if he would like a play date with any of the children. Those are the children whose parents you want to meet.

Step 2: Introduce Yourself

The first time you see the child's mom, a brief introduction is fine. It gives the other mom a chance to ask her child if he is interested in playing with your child—for example: "Hi, I'm Joan—Tommy's mom. My son is always talking about how much he likes to play with your son at school, so I thought I'd introduce myself."

You are doing this to test the waters—to see how interested the other parent is. Think about how enthusiastic she was at this introduction. If she wasn't interested, don't pursue her. Sometimes a mom will warm up after she has thought about it for a while or asked her child about his interest in your child.

Remember that most moms want to do the same thing you are doing for the same reasons. You'll know when you pick the right mom because it will be easier than you think!

Step 3: Continue Chatting

Once you've introduced yourself, it's important to get to know the other mom better immediately if the other mom seems receptive. Begin chatting during child exchange and pickup times. If it is difficult for you to talk to other moms, there are two approaches.

PLAN A

The mom you want to get to know better is talking to one or two other moms. Read the first part of Chapter Seven about rules of etiquette for joining others. These may also apply in this situation to get you into conversations with other moms.

PLAN B

The mom you want to get to know better is alone. You might think of a few possible things you can say to her so you won't get flustered in the moment. Avoid yes-no questions; open-ended questions keep the conversation going. Here are some suggestions as to what to say to start the conversation rolling:

- Compliment the other mom's child, but ask a question to help the conversation continue: "Your son swims very well. Did he have classes?" "Olivia's dress is really cute. Where did you get it?"

- Keep it relevant to the context where the kids know each other: "So what do you think of the new teacher's aide?" "Are you going to the T-ball game on Saturday?"

- Ask a few easy get-to-know-you questions: "What other sports does Sam do?" "Do you have any other kids?" "Where is Sydney going for first grade?" "Do you live nearby?"

Step 4: Assess the Response from the Other Mom

If you have picked a receptive mom to approach, the conversation flows easily for her and you, and there is mutual warmth. Perhaps she gladly answers your questions and reciprocates with questions of her own. If the other mom is not receptive, wait for a pause and say, "It was very nice meeting you," and walk away.

Step 5: Continue the Conversation While Checking Out the Other Mom

You may suggest going for coffee while your children are at their dance or karate lesson to keep the conversation going. Remember that your goal is to assess if you are comfortable with her, not to try to make friends. Does she seem responsible? Does she appear to be without serious quirks? Does she keep you in your comfort zone by not getting too personal too quickly? If the answers to these questions are yes, then proceed to the next step. Otherwise you can always say how happy you were to talk and walk on.

Step 6: Introduce the Idea of a Play Date

Here are two examples:

- "Do you think it would be a good idea for our kids to get together for a play date sometime?"

- "I'd be happy to have Sarah over to our house for a play date with Rebecca sometime. Is that something you would be interested in?"

Step 7: Make an Invitation for a Specific Time and Day

If you suggested the idea, wait for the other mom to make a specific invitation for the first play date.

PLAN A

The other mom gets to the specifics right away: "How about Thursday?" You can then work out a mutually convenient day and time on the spot. Get the other mom's phone number, and call to finalize the play date. (See Chapter Twelve for tips on having the play date.)

PLAN B

The other mom was not specific. Many moms won't say no because they won't want to hurt your feelings or they are unsure of the suitability of a play date. Instead they will keep things vague with a statement such as, "Yes, we'll have to get them together sometime." Accept this, as things may work out later. However, at this point it is up to the other mom to make the next approach.

The Next Step

You saw how easy it was to start networking because you know the steps and many parents have the same goals as you do. The next step is setting up play dates (Chapter Twelve). However, if your child has difficulty meeting other kids, read Chapter Seven, or has difficulty being a good sport, read Chapter Eight. If he has difficulty being a good host, read Chapter Thirteen.

PART TWO

Making Friends

—•—

A good friend is someone who is considerate of your child's feelings, someone whom she can trust to confide in. To have a good friend, your child must learn to be a good friend. You can help teach your child how to go about this.

7

Joining Others at Play

———•———

The Problem

- My child is uncomfortable meeting other children. How do I help?
- My child can meet other children but soon alienates them. Can I help?

Background: Making a Good First Impression

You will almost never see a child meet new children by introducing himself and shaking hands. Children make new acquaintances by joining others who are playing.[1] Some children don't know how to do this and avoid it. Others join in but do it in a way that quickly alienates others. This chapter shows you how to help your child meet new friends and make good first impressions—one of the most important social skills children can learn.

Rules of Etiquette for Joining Others

Try this at the next party you attend. Stand near two people you might be interested in meeting who are talking to each other. Look at them and say nothing; just listen. If they are talking about something interesting, stick around. If not, move on. Notice you don't hurt anyone's feelings if you move on.

If you're still hanging around, notice whether the people conversing start looking at you while they're talking. If they do, they have invited you into their conversation ("opened the circle"). If they don't look at you, they probably want to be alone. Notice again that you don't hurt anyone's feelings when you walk away. Rules of etiquette protect everyone's feelings.

Studies show that children use three approaches when near other children at play.[2] Some follow five rules of etiquette and easily join others. Some children break these rules: although they may join others, they quickly alienate them. Still other children don't know these rules and don't try to join others. This group winds up playing by themselves. How children join is shown in Table 7.1.

During one of my interviews with children, a well-liked seven-year-old girl surprised me (and her mother sitting nearby) by reciting all of the five rules without any help. In my interviews with girls and their mothers, I learned two other rules that girls have to follow to join other girls at play:

1. If you know a girl playing in a game you would like to join, you first look at her. If she looks back at you, then you ask her if you may join the game.
2. If she doesn't look at you, she is letting you know you shouldn't join.

Where and When

Many parents think it's okay for their child to try to meet others anywhere and at any time. In fact, it is better to encourage your child to try to make friends only at certain times and places. Studies show that children who try to make friends when the teacher or coach is talking or other children are trying to work

Table 7.1 How Children Join Others at Play

Follows the Five Rules of Etiquette	Doesn't Know Rules of Etiquette and Doesn't Join	Breaks Rules of Etiquette
1. Watches the other children playing to show that he is interested. Figures out the game rules and who is winning. Checks that the skill level of the children playing is about the same as his.	Off by himself; doesn't watch others or watches from too far away.	Starts playing without knowing the game, attempts to disrupt the game, or annoys other children by asking what they are playing.
2. Watches silently or says something nice about children playing: "Nice shot," "Nice try."	Doesn't watch closely enough.	Criticizes the children playing: "You stupid jerk! Don't you know how to play?"
3. Waits for a pause in the game before asking to join.	Waits to be asked; never asks to join.	Barges in and begins playing.
4. Boy: Asks to join the side that needs more help (the losing side or side with fewer players). Girl: Asks the girl who owns the rope or ball to join.	Never asks to join.	Boy: Joins the winning side, if he knows which side that is. Girl: Tries to make the others let her in: "If you don't let me play, I'll tell the teacher."
5. Accepts no for an answer if not allowed to join.		Complains if told he can't join.

in the classroom do not make friends.[3] Potential playmates reject these advances not only because they might get in trouble, but they are usually annoyed when someone distracts them from their activity. Better times and places to try to make friends are when children are waiting or unoccupied, for instance, before or after school, before or after team practice on playgrounds, or in lunchroom.

I've found the steps set out in the next section to be effective for boys and girls who are in first grade or older (below first grade, children do not organize themselves in games). Boys will want to join other boys when they are playing, while girls are successful at joining either girls or boys. Children who master all the steps will have skills to make them successful in joining others at play in any situation.

Solving the Problem: Joining Children in Play

Familiarize yourself with the five rules of etiquette in the left-hand column of Table 7.1 and how children break them. Coach your child about how to meet other children and make good first impressions. It will take more than one session for younger children to use these rules effectively. Inevitably your child will make errors and will do some things well. You are watching for improvement from session to session. I find that children are very interested in learning these rules. Remember that your role here is to teach and support your child, not do it for your child.

Step 1: Search Your Neighborhood for a Suitable Public Place

Find a place in your neighborhood where several groups of children the same age or a little younger than your child play. A local playground or a school yard in your neighborhood where children gather and organize their own games are the best bets. Find a safe place where you are comfortable with the children who are playing. Do this at least a day before you try step 2.

Step 2: Teach Your Child the Steps to Joining Other Children

Younger children join others while they are playing. Children older than eleven years old join others when they are conversing. Here's how Dad introduces the rules to his eleven-year-old son Seth (who is a bit testy about the whole idea):

DAD: Humor me, and remember some rules for when you want to join in on some kids playing a game or talking.

SETH: What if they're talking about gangs?

DAD: First, listen to them when they're talking. Listen closely enough so they know you're interested.

SETH: What if I see a gun in their pocket? Can I say, "Is that a 38 or a 45?"

DAD: You wait and listen and see if you are interested in what they're saying.

SETH: They'll just tell me to go away.

DAD: You look at their eyes. If they look at you while they're talking, chances are they are asking you to join in.

SETH: I did that the other day. I waited until they were through, and I knew one of them. I started talking to the one I didn't know.

DAD: Look at their eyes: that's how people tell you they are interested in you. It took me a long time to figure that out. Then you wait for a pause in the conversation.

SETH: What if they talk very fast and don't take a breath?

DAD: Then you don't say anything. Wait for your chance, and say something to help them converse.

Younger children require a simplified version of this so they will remember the rules:

1. Watch the game for the rules.
2. Wait for a pause in the game.
3. Ask to join.
4. If they say no, look for another game.

Here's how Mom teaches seven-year-old Rachel to join:

MOM: We're going to watch some children playing. You might want to play with them, so I'm going to tell you some rules that will help you ask them to join. Let's say you see three girls playing with a ball. The first thing you do is watch. What are you watching for?

RACHEL: I don't know.

MOM: You're watching to see what game they are playing and if you might like the kids and the game. The next thing you do is wait. What might you be waiting for?

RACHEL: The end of the game?

MOM: Yes! Either the end of the game or a break in the game. Then you ask. What do you ask?

RACHEL: "Can I play?"

MOM: That's right. Let's say one side is doing better than the other. You would ask the side that's not doing as well because they might need your help. Remember: watch, wait. and ask. Okay?

RACHEL: Okay.

Step 3: Along with Your Child, Watch a Group of Children at Play

Bring a newspaper or magazine along with you. Have your child pick a group of children at play. Encourage her to pick children who appear to be the same age or slightly younger and about the same skill level or slightly less skilled than your child:

- Pick children who are about as skilled as your child at the game they are playing.

- Don't pick older children because they are less likely to accept your child as an equal.

- Don't pick children your child already knows, which will interfere with your teaching.

- Don't criticize your child in any way as he tries to join.

You and your child begin by watching a game in play from about five or ten feet away (the more running around in the game, the farther away your child watches). Watching a game from the sidelines is the way your child gets information and lets the other children know she wants to play. Sometimes the children playing will ask onlookers to join.

You may stand alongside your child in this step to make sure she understands the game. Don't be disappointed if your child isn't asked to play. It's important for her to learn the correct steps so that she doesn't intrude on other children's play.

Children who are having fun playing are usually annoyed by being asked what they are playing. They are also irritated by children who join a game but don't know what's going on. Have your child whisper to you what the children are playing, what the rules are, if there are teams, who is winning (for girls, ask if she knows who brought the toy the children are playing with), and any other details of the game that are important.

Here's how a dad coaches his son, Lee:

DAD: [Pointing to five children at play in the distance] Do those kids look interesting to play with?

LEE: I don't know.

DAD: Let's stay here and watch what they're doing. Let's look at those kids first. See if you can tell me what they're playing and what the rules are. [They watch for five minutes, and Lee correctly answers what game it is, who is on which team, who is winning.] That's great. You understand what's happening. Which side would need your help more?

LEE: The side with only two kids on it. The other side has three.

DAD: That's right!

This is an important question and answer. Your child needs to be looking to join the side that needs the most help, not the side that's winning. The children who are already playing will welcome help (that is, if your child's skill level is about the same as the children playing the game), since it evens up the game and makes it more fun for all.

Step 4: Help Your Child Think of How to Join In

Dad will help Lee think about how to join the game by focusing on two things Lee needs to know: when to ask to join and what to say. A pause in the game or the end of a round are ideal times to ask to join because they do not interrupt the flow of the game and show the children at play that Lee is considerate and knowledgeable about the game:

DAD: Which side will you ask to join?
LEE: The side with only two on it.
DAD: That's right. What can you ask them?
LEE: Do you need another guy on your team?
DAD: That sounds great. When would be a good time to ask?
LEE: After someone scores a basket.
DAD: That might work!

For girls, add:

MOM: Whose ball is it?
LAURA: It's that girl's [pointing].

MOM: That's right. So who would you ask if you wanted to play?

LAURA: The girl whose ball it is.

MOM: Great!

Step 5: Review with Your Child Why Children Are Kept Out of a Game

Being turned down from games is a fact of life. Table 7.2 lists reasons I commonly find for children being turned down and what to do about each.

Children without friendship problems are turned down frequently and are not concerned by it (this also shows the children at play that the child will consider their wishes even if it means the child doesn't get to play).[4] Your child should expect to be

Table 7.2   Getting Turned Down

Reasons for Being Turned Down	What to Do About It
You did something to them before (avoided them, gotten them in trouble with the teacher).	Treat others as you would have them treat you. Choose another group to join.
You tried to join in the wrong way.	Next time, watch first and praise other kids. Wait for a pause in the action to ask to join.
They are too popular, too athletic, not interested in the same things you are.	Pick children close in skill and interests to your own.
They don't want to make new friends.	Pick other children.
They misunderstood what you wanted to do.	Say it differently; for example, point out that they have two fewer kids on their side.
They didn't feel like playing with you just then.	Try again later.

turned down about half the time he attempts to join others. Far from being a crushing event, being turned down should get your child to look for another group of children who are playing. Prepare your child for this before he attempts to join in. You can do this by speaking about "another child":

DAD: Why might those kids not want another boy to play?
LEE: I don't know.
DAD: Suppose the boy was mean to them before.
LEE: Then they probably wouldn't like him and wouldn't let him play.
DAD: Yeah. What other reasons might they have?
LEE: Maybe they just didn't like him.
DAD: Maybe they knew he played much better than they did.
LEE: Yeah.
DAD: Maybe they didn't want to meet anyone new.
LEE: Yeah.
DAD: What's the best thing you could do if some boys don't want to play with you just when you want to?
LEE: I don't know.
DAD: Which one sounds good to you: try other kids, or try again later? [They're both good alternatives.]
LEE: Try other kids.
DAD: That's a good choice. Who else will you try of the kids we are watching?
LEE: [Pointing] Those kids playing handball.
DAD: Yes!

Dad is encouraging Lee to solve this for himself, but when he doesn't know the answer, Dad gives him a choice of two alternatives. This keeps Lee involved in the process of discovery. It also gives Lee the idea that there are always options other than joining those particular children.

Step 6: Coach Your Child to Praise Other Children's Behavior

You are teaching your child how to let others at play tactfully know that he is interested in joining. One powerful way to do this is for him to praise the other children. Children who receive praise themselves are more likely to praise others. If you have started using tactful praise (Chapter Three) and if you praise your child for trying his best now, it is more likely that he will praise others. Praise is contagious.

Examples of praise your child can use for the children he is watching are "nice try" (for a near-basket) or "great shot" (for a basket).

DAD: [Waiting until a child playing almost gets a basket] What is something nice you can say about that shot?
LEE: I don't know.
DAD: How about, "Nice try!" Tell me when you can say something nice about what one of the kids in the game does. [Another child makes a good shot, and Lee says nothing.]
LEE: Oh yeah. [calls out] "Nice shot!"
DAD: Right!

This is hard for some children to do. Go on to step 7 even if your child doesn't get this step.

Step 7: Encourage Your Child to Try to Join

The other way your child tactfully shows interest in joining is to move to just outside the group at play. Getting this close sends the message to the children at play that your child is interested in this game. Encourage your child to ask to join after he correctly tells you when and who he will ask to play:

DAD: See if the kids will let you play. Go ahead and get closer to them. Stand over there and watch them [pointing to the sidelines of the game]. I'll be sitting over at that bench over there [pointing].

LEE: Okay. [Dad now backs away about ten more feet, sits on a nearby bench, and pretends to read a newspaper while actually watching.]

Step 8: End Your Child's Participation

You want to have your child end his participation on a good note. If he generally gets along well with others, then allow him to play until the game ends.

If he frequently gets into arguments with others, allow him to play only for about ten minutes until he learns the rules of a good sport (set out in the next chapter). Here's how Mom tactfully pulls Laura out of the game:

MOM: [Walking up close to where Laura joined some other girls at play] I'm sorry, Laura. We're going to have to leave soon. I need to do some errands.

LAURA: Oh, Mom, I just started playing!

MOM: I'm sorry. You can play with these girls again the next time we're here.

LAURA: Can I finish my next turn?

MOM: That's okay with me. Ask the girls if it is okay.

If your child wasn't successful at joining, praise her for trying. Remind your child that five out of every ten times, everyone gets turned down. Here's an example in which a group of girls did not let Laura join:

MOM: How did it go?

LAURA: They said no when I asked if I could play.

MOM: You looked as if you were doing the steps well. I'm glad you listened to them and went away.

Laura's mom has Laura repeat steps 1 to 6 with another group of children.

Step 9: Privately Praise Your Child

Praise your child for attempts to follow your advice whether or not the attempts were successful.

PLAN A

Your child was successful. Here's an example in which Lee has just finished playing well with a group of children he has joined:

DAD: [Still pretending to read a magazine when Lee comes up to him] You did a good job following the steps to joining—it worked that time! I liked how you looked interested in the game the kids were playing before you asked to join.

PLAN B

Your child was not successful. Lee watched the other kids playing and asked to join them, but they ignored him.

DAD: [Still pretending to read a magazine, when Lee comes up to him] Well, you did everything you needed to do: you watched, then waited for a good time. I liked how you were able to take no for an answer. That showed the other kids that you were considerate of their wishes. What could you do now?

LEE: Try other kids?

DAD: That's right! Let's see who else looks interesting to play with [starts the process over again].

• • •

I have summarized the steps to teach your child how to join in.

✓ *Checklist for Joining Other Children at Play* ✓

Step 1: Search your neighborhood for a suitable public place where groups of children the same age or a little younger than your child play.

Step 2: Teach your child the steps to joining other children:

1. Listen or watch close enough so they know you're interested. Figure out what they are playing and their skill level.
2. Watch silently or praise, for example, say, "Nice shot!"
3. Wait for a pause in the game.
4. Boys: Ask to join the side that needs the most help; Girls: Ask the girl who owns the toy.
5. Accept no for an answer if they turn you down.

Step 3: With your child, watch a group of children at play.

- Pick children who appear to be the same age or slightly younger and about the same skill level or slightly less skilled than your child.
- Watch from five or ten feet away.
- Make sure your child know the rules, who is winning, and who needs more help (and for girls, who brought the game).

Step 4: Help your child think of how to join in:

- Wait for a pause in the game or the end of a round.
- Have your child rehearse what he is going to say.

Step 5: Review with your child why children are kept out of a game. The bottom line is take no for an answer and move on.

Step 6: Coach your child to praise other children's behavior.

Step 7: Encourage your child to try to join. Move to just outside the group at play. You move back to a bench to pretend to read your newspaper.

Step 8: End your child's participation if your child was successful at joining.

> Plan A: If you child generally gets along well with others, allow her to play until the game ends.

> Plan B: If your child frequently gets into arguments with other children, allow her to play only for about ten minutes. (Read Chapter Eight for the rules of a good sport.)

Step 9: Privately praise your child for attempts to follow your advice, whether or not the attempts were successful.

The Next Step

Your child now has a much better chance of meeting others and making a good first impression even when you're not around. If your child plays well with others, repeat these steps several times to get her comfortable with her new skill. She might be able to get the telephone numbers from those other children (you'll use them to help your child start making close friends in Chapter Ten). If your child has difficulty being considerate in group games and quickly alienates others, then go on to the next chapter to teach her the rules of a good sport.

8

Becoming a Good Sport

———•———

The Problem

- How can I get my child to argue and brag less during games?

Background: Keeping Others as Playmates

Once a year, my Cub Scout pack has its annual Pinewood Derby. The Cubs race cars that they and their dads build. Everyone gets a prize—participation, best design, most unusual—but only one wins the derby.

My first year as Cub master, I was particularly struck by several Cubs who cried when they lost. They were supposed to be having fun! I decided that the reason they were feeling miserable was that no one told them to have fun rather than to try to win.

The next year, I started off the event by telling them they were there to have fun and to show that they could be a good sport. Only one Cub would win. No one cried this time. Being a good sport was as important as winning to those kids. The main point of this chapter is to prevent poor sportsmanship by having children set different priorities.

Table 8.1   How Winning at All Costs Differs from Being a Good Sport

Good Sport	Winning at All Costs
Takes the game seriously (but not too seriously; after all, it's only a game)	Clowns around (for example, steals the ball and doesn't give it back)
Follows the rules of the game	Frequently breaks the rules
Lets other children have a good time by staying in position and waiting his turn	Tries to play all positions (a "ball hog") and doesn't let others have a turn
Avoids arguments	Gets angry, gets into arguments, plays "referee" (saying, for example, "You stepped on the line. You're out!")
Stays until the end of the game	Walks away when losing or tired of playing

Chapter Seven helped you teach your child how to start playing with others without one strike against him because of the way he entered the game. If he constantly squabbles with other children, then he probably is playing to win at all costs and isn't thinking about keeping others as playmates. Table 8.1 lists the ways a good sport plays differently from the child who plays to win at all costs.

You saw in the previous chapter how joining others at play is a skill that children can and like to learn. It's the same with being a good sport. Children who don't follow rules of etiquette usually don't know them. You may be surprised that the child who plays to win at all costs is glad when someone teaches him this valuable lesson in life.

Solving the Problem: Teaching Good Sportsmanship

Return to the park or playground where you successfully practiced the steps set out in Chapter Seven. This time you will need at least three good sport sessions to teach your child additional rules of etiquette: the rules of a good sport.

If your child sees some of the children he was successful joining recently, he can approach them again. You stopped them from playing last time in order to leave on a good note. Now comes the payoff for doing this. Begin by following the first six steps below.

Step 1: Bring an Icebreaker Toy and a Magazine for You to Pretend to Read

Your child should still try the techniques learned in the last chapter to join others at play. If other children aren't already playing when you arrive at your playground or park, your child should be ready to start playing anyway by bringing an icebreaker toy.

Clarisse, age eight, brought a Chinese jump rope to school. When two other girls saw what she had, they immediately wanted to play with her. Since it was her rope, she could make the rules simple enough so that she could have fun. They all had fun for the entire twenty minutes of recess.

Bringing a toy to public places can break the ice. The outside toys you picked in Chapter Three are ideal for this:

- Bring a ball, jump rope, or chalk (for girls, for hopscotch).
- Don't bring one-at-a-time activities like video games, drawing materials, radio-controlled cars, or books.
- Don't bring violent activities like ninja weapons, toy guns, water pistols, or any toys that shoot projectiles.

Step 2: Teach the Rules of a Good Sport

It will be impossible for your child to abide by these rules and try to win at all costs. Problems playing with others will disappear. I list the rules in the best order to teach them, and then I'll show you how.

Rules of a Good Sport

1. *Take the game seriously—no clowning around.* A child who clowns around when others are taking a game seriously makes a poor first impression.

2. *No refereeing.* Refereeing means pointing out rule violations ("You got there after I tagged you"), or criticizing others ("That was a stupid thing to do").

3. *Let others have fun too.* Even if your child is better than the other players at a particular sport, the idea is for everyone to have fun. Your child should stay in his own area and wait his turn, not try to catch any balls that someone else could catch or take too long for his turn.

4. *Praise other children.* Examples are "great shot" and "nice try," and giving the high-five to members of one's team.

5. *If bored, suggest a change in activity or switching positions.* Examples are, "How about if I hit the ball and you catch for a while?" or, "Could we play for just five minutes more? I'm getting tired."

6. *Suggest a new rule instead of arguing.* For example, instead of saying, "That was a foul. You're out!" an alternative is, "Let's make a rule that the foul line [pointing to it] is a take-over. Okay?" The child then accepts either a yes or no answer and abides by it.

7. *If you win, pretend that winning wasn't important to you.*

8. *Do not walk away from a game when you are losing or tired of playing.* Stay until the end of a round so you don't leave the side uneven.

Don't try to teach all of these rules in one session. Make sure your child knows the first four.

Talk to your child about the rules of a good sport before beginning to play the first time. While you are on your way to the good sport session is a good time. Make sure there are no distractions, such as your car radio, and then briefly review the rules:

DAD: We're heading for the same park where we met those kids last time. I want you to remember four rules of a good sport: let other kids play their own positions, no clowning around, let someone else be the referee, and try to say "good shot" or "nice try" to the other kids. Okay?

KEITH: Okay.

DAD: What were the four rules?

KEITH: Let other kids play their own positions, don't clown around, let someone else referee, and what else?

DAD: Try saying things like "good shot," or "nice try," like you did last time, okay?

KEITH: Okay.

Step 3: Encourage Your Child to Attempt to Join

Your child should use the joining steps from the previous chapter until he is accepted into a group so that you can do your good sport coaching. He should stand on the sidelines, within ten feet, watching others in play. If he has brought a toy, he gives it to you to hold. You watch from twenty to thirty feet away. If your child is turned down, he should try to join other children or should start playing with the toy that he brought. If another child approaches while he's playing with the toy, he should ask him to play.

Step 4: See That Your Child Follows the Rules of a Good Sport

Continue to watch from afar. Relax and pretend to read that magazine. You're not really reading, of course, but watching your child. You are looking to see

- That your child follows the rules of a good sport. You will be praising him for this in private after the game.
- That your child doesn't break a good sport rule you've taught her.
- Instances where you have to teach her rules 5 to 8.

PLAN A

Your child occasionally breaks a good sport rule you have taught him. Remember that old habits die hard. It's only natural that your child will occasionally break a good sport rule. Come up to where the children are playing. Take him aside immediately, and quietly remind him in a neutral tone of voice of the broken rule. Although reminding your child in this way disrupts the game and may frustrate the other children, I have found that the other children will continue playing and ignore what's going on. They're more interested in the game than what's happening to your child. Remember that your goal here is to instruct your child so he can return to play and successfully apply the rule:

MOM: [Walking up to Laura] Laura, I need to speak to you for a moment.

LAURA: I'm playing right now.

MOM: Come over here for a minute, please.

LAURA: [Comes, with complaining voice] What, Mom?

MOM: [Whispering] Thanks for coming over. Remember the rules of a good sport?

LAURA: Yeah.

MOM: What are they?

LAURA: Let other kids play their own positions, and I don't remember the rest.

MOM: Take the game seriously, let someone else be the referee, and try to say a couple of nice things to the others.

LAURA: Oh yeah.

MOM: You need to let someone else be the referee. Let someone else point out when someone trips on the jump rope. Can you do that?

LAURA: Yes, Mom.

MOM: Okay, you can go back to play now.

At first Laura will need several reminders like this. But after several good sport sessions, following the rules becomes a habit.

PLAN B

Your child breaks a rule you haven't told him yet. Introduce new rules as instances come up. For example, when you see your child having an argument, immediately take your child aside. In a neutral tone, whisper the sixth rule of a good sport:

DAD: [Taking Keith over to one side after the beginning of an argument over where the foul line is] I want to tell you about another rule of a good sport: instead of arguing, suggest a new rule.

KEITH: But he hit the ball out of bounds!

DAD: Just ask him if you can have a new rule. Say, "How about we make that the foul line?" If he doesn't want to, then you will have to accept where he says the foul line is. Can you do that?

KEITH: Why do I have to?

DAD: You need to be a good sport so the game will be more fun for everyone.

KEITH: Okay.

DAD: Thanks. Now you can go back and play.

If Keith refused, then Dad would take him out of the game until he agrees to follow the rules of a good sport.

Step 5: Don't Let Your Child End the Game Unless His Playmates Agree

Your child should not walk away from a game when he is losing or tired of playing. He needs to be considerate of everyone's feelings. In addition, other children are counting on your child to help them play the game. This is how it's done:

KEITH: [Leaving the game while others still want to play] I don't want to play anymore.

DAD: [Walking to Keith from his bench] Keith, ask the other boys and see if they want to stop.

KEITH: But I'm tired of playing.

DAD: You still need to check with them. That's being considerate of their feelings. What do you ask them?

KEITH: "Is it okay if we stop?"

Step 6: Praise Your Child

If your child was able to follow any rule of a good sport, praise him about it—but in private, after the game:

DAD: [On the way home from the park] I liked the way you took the game seriously. I think all the kids had a good time playing together.

If your child had trouble following the rules, proceed to step 7.

Step 7: Make a Pact with Your Child Before the Next Good Sport Session

Immediately before a good sport session, make a deal with your child. Offer a small reward that you can give easily and immediately after the session. If the rules were broken seven times in the previous good sport session, offer a reward for three or fewer infractions this time:

DAD: Before you play with those children, remember the four rules of a good sport?

KEITH: What rules?

DAD: Let other kids play their own positions, take the game seriously, let someone else be the referee, and try to say a couple of nice things to the others.

KEITH: Okay.

DAD: It's been hard for you to remember them. How about a special treat if you remember today?

KEITH: Could we go for ice cream?

DAD: It's a deal. If I remind you fewer than four times about the rules, then we will go for ice cream.

Dad removes Keith from the activity after each time Keith forgets a good sport rule and lets him return after he has promised to follow the rule. If Dad has to remind Keith three or fewer times, Keith gets the ice cream. If you have made a pact with your child, don't count the first time rules 5 to 8 are broken.

If Keith has to be reminded more than three times, then Dad tells him that next time he can try again, but this time they skip the ice cream. Next time Dad makes the play time shorter (reducing it from a half-hour to twenty minutes) and makes the same pact with Keith: he takes Keith out for ice cream if there are three or fewer infractions.

• • •

I have summarized the steps to teach your child how to be a good sport.

✓ *Good Sport Sessions Checklist* ✓

Step 1: Bring an icebreaker toy and a magazine for you to pretend to read.

- Bring a ball, jump rope, or chalk (for girls, for hopscotch).
- Don't bring one-at-a time activities like video games, drawing materials, radio-controlled cars, or books.
- Don't bring violent activities like ninja weapons, toy guns, water pistols, or any toys that shoot projectiles.

Step 2: Teach the rules of a good sport. Teach the first four (for younger children) or first four to six (older children):

1. Take the game seriously—no clowning around.
2. No refereeing.
3. Let others have fun too.
4. Praise other children.
5. If you are bored, suggest a change in activity or switching positions.
6. Suggest a new rule instead of arguing.
7. If you win, pretend that winning wasn't important to you.
8. Do not walk away from a game when you are losing or tired of playing.

Step 3: Encourage your child to attempt to join.

- He should stand on the sidelines, within ten feet, watching others in play.
- If he has brought a toy, he gives it to you to hold.
- You watch from twenty to thirty feet away.
- If your child is turned down, he should try to join other children or should start playing with the toy he brought.

- If another child approaches while he's playing with the toy, he should ask him to play.

Step 4: See that your child follows the rules of a good sport.

- Continue to watch from afar that your child follows the rules of a good sport.
- Look for instances where you have to teach her rules 5 to 8.

  Plan A: Your child occasionally breaks a good sport rule you have taught him: Take him aside immediately and quietly remind him of the broken rule.

  Plan B: Your child breaks a rule you haven't told him yet. Introduce new rules as instances come up.

Step 5: Don't let your child end the game unless his playmates agree.

Step 6: Praise your child in private after the game if he was able to follow any rule of a good sport.

The Next Step

Repeat the good sport sessions until your child is able to abide by all the rules of a good sport for two sessions. When this happens, congratulate yourself because your child is making good first impressions. The other children may want to get to know your child better. Chapter Nine helps you guide your child to look for closer friends.

9

Looking for Closer Friends and Joining a Friendship Group

———•———

The Problem

- My daughter feels left out of a group of four girlfriends at her school. How can I help?
- My son has no close friends. What can I do about this?

Background: Friendship Groups

As elementary school children mature, they relate to their close friends more deeply. To first graders, a close friend is anyone they play with, especially anyone they have play dates with. They become selective in their close friends by second grade and begin to have special interests by fourth grade. Fifth and sixth graders are most intimate with their same-sex friends before their interest in the opposite sex begins to distract them. You can see this in Table 9.1.

The Value of Friendship Groups

Three times as many boys as girls enroll in my Children's Friendship Training classes. It seems that far fewer girls than boys have friendship problems. Part of the reason may be that many more girls than boys belong to friendship groups. A friendship group includes one's

Table 9.1 Development of Close Friendships

Grade	What They Do with Close Friends	How They View Close Friends
Kindergarten and first grade	They will play with anyone. Closer friends are determined by how often they get together after school.	Close friends share activities and toys.
Second and third grades	Boys and girls publicly avoid each other. Close friends begin to cooperate and adjust to each others' actions and thoughts. Boys: Start to organize into small group games with rules. They form temporary clubs with a leader. Girls: Four or five friends sometimes become a friendship group.	Close friends are constant companions.
Fourth grade	Specialized interests begin to emerge. Boys: Small groups begin to hang around with each other. Girls: Friendship groups are more constant and begin to center on interests: bike riding, ballet, theater group, and so on.	Close friends have common interests, likes and dislikes, similar abilities, and compatible personalities.
Fifth grade	Boys: Hang around exclusively with a group of other boys with similar interests. Girls: Longer telephone calls and sharing secrets make their debut.	Close friends are intimate and support each other.
Sixth grade	Boys: Conversation begins to play a larger part in their get-togethers. Girls: Have telephone calls for conversation rather than information.	Close friends "really understand" each other.

best friend as well as several of one's closer but not best friends. Girls' friendship groups (when they belong to one) are closer and smaller than boys' friendship groups.[1] Boys have one or two best friends, which changes from time to time, but usually stays within four or five constant closer friends.

Jeremy, Greg, and Steven, who have known each other since kindergarten, are an example of an ideal friendship group of boys. They live within two blocks of each other and have had many individual play dates with each other. Each occasionally plays with other boys who aren't part of their group.

In fourth grade, their parents feel confident that they can safely cross small streets. The boys then get together as a group after the parents confer with each other on the phone. Jeremy and Steven ride their bikes to Greg's house and play there for a while. They tell Greg's mom they are going to ride their bikes for forty-five minutes, and she makes sure they return. After they return, they head over to Steven's house, where his mom has planned to give them lunch.

Here is an account of an ideal girls' friendship group. Four mothers make frequent play dates with each other for their second-grade daughters. The mothers also find that they like each other. When the girls are in third grade, the mothers go out for coffee after they drop their girls off for the horseback riding lessons that all their girls take together. Many girls fantasize about having friendship groups like these four girls had because it formed quickly, lasted a long time, and involved the parents. Many girls want special friends, or "sisters."

Here is a more typical account. For the past three years, six-year-old Julie has attended a ballet class. She has met several girls there, but only Ginger remains her long-time friend. Julie meets Jolene in third grade when they both began to ride the same bus to school. She met Emily at Girl Scout camp and also in the city orchestra. In sixth grade, Julie, Ginger, Jolene, and Emily attend the same middle school. They all eat lunch together every day at school and have slumber parties once every couple of months. Their common interests are intellectual (they are all in honors classes) and watching movies at their slumber parties.

Girls' typical friendship groups form slowly by adding individual girls and then suddenly may coalesce when circumstances change, usually at the beginning of a school year. Children pick each other to be friends on an individual basis through common interests. The parents know each other but are not necessarily friends.

Another pattern that is common among girls (about 39 percent of girls) is they don't belong to a circle of girls who are mutual friends.[2] Instead, they have best friends in many of the activities they join—a best friend in their dance class, a best friend in the neighborhood, and a best friend in school, for example. I believe that either of these patterns is beneficial for girls' long-term adjustment. The trouble is that some girls are unhappy unless they belong to a friendship group.

The one type of friendship group to avoid is the one that is labeled by most as the "popular kids" (but not well-liked kids). Members of this group value being particularly exclusive.[3] This type of group has a dominant leader who allows others in or excludes others. Children entering into this type of group are forced to give up their previous friends, usually through negative comments from group members. Parents can tell that their child is entering such a group when they hear that group members are pressuring their child to give up their old friends.

Solving the Problem: Help Your Child Have a Few Close Friends

While it is not necessary for boys or girls to belong to a friendship group, it is desirable to have two to four close friends of the same sex. Girls and boys can make rewarding playmates for each other, and nothing I am about to say is intended to discourage you from helping your child maintain these opposite-sex friendships.

However, it is important for children to have same-sex closer friends since they will have playmates to play with in public places like the school yard.

Step 1: Ask Your Child About Favored Playmates

Find out from your child who she is spending time with at school:

> Mom: What did you do today at recess?
> Danielle: I played hopscotch.
> Mom: With whom?
> Danielle: Trisha and Joy.
> Mom: Do you usually play with them?
> Danielle: Yes.
> Mom: Do you want to have either of them over to the house?
> Danielle: Yes.

If your child does not have favored playmates at school, ask about after-school or neighborhood activities. If there are no playmates in any of these activities, follow the steps in Chapters Four through Six to help your child meet new friends.

Some children complain that they are being excluded from a particular friendship group they want to join. I feel it is a mistake for a parent to encourage a child to try to join a friendship group. Children who are complaining about not being included in a specific friendship group are

- Trying for a friendship group for the wrong reasons—popularity or status—rather than looking for children with common interests who would make the best playmates.
- Trying to be accepted too quickly into a friendship group—trying to get all the children in the group to include them at once—rather than seeking to establish separate friendships with each child. Establishing

separate friendships is the best way to join a larger friendship group.[4]

Mom finds out her daughter Kate is being left out of a friendship group at school:

KATE: I don't have anyone at school to hang out with.
MOM: What about Evelyn? You play with her after church.
KATE: Evelyn is too busy with Abby and Sharon to talk to me at school.

If Mom decides with Kate that common interests are not strong enough with Abby or Sharon, Kate needs to look elsewhere for friends she can hang out with at school. Mom helps her do this:

MOM: Is there anyone else you like at school?
KATE: I like Monica, but she's not friends with Evelyn, Abby, or Sharon.
MOM: It's up to Evelyn, Abby, and Sharon if they want to hang out with you. Meanwhile, don't depend on them. Do you like Monica enough to ask her over?

If the answer is yes, then it's time for a play date. If something didn't gel with Evelyn, Abby, or Sharon, then maybe something better will happen with Monica. Otherwise Kate keeps looking for additional friends. Remember that it is not essential that your child belong to any friendship group, but it is important for her to have close friends.

Step 2: Linger for a Few Minutes Before or After School and Activities

Arrive a few minutes before the activity is over and watch from the sidelines to see whom your child is hanging around (read Chapter Six for more help):

Mom: [After watching her son, Alex, talking to another boy] Hi, Alex. Who was that boy you were talking to?

Alex: That was Jeffrey.

Mom: Does Jeffrey play with you at school?

Alex: Yes, we played handball at recess today.

Mom: Would you like to invite him over to our house?

Alex: Yes.

The next day Alex's mother can strike up a conversation with Jeffrey's mom before they pick up their sons (see Chapter Six for more help with this).

Step 3: Arrange Play Dates with One Child at a Time

You have a common interest with some parents: both of your children want to play together. You have found out who these children are in the last step; now meet their parents to arrange play dates. Although in-person arrangements are always better for first and second graders, telephoning can also be effective, especially for older children who will make the call (see the next chapter). Talk to whichever parent is picking up your child's desired playmate at school.

Here is an example of how making friends with one child at a time works, even if the girls start out by being hesitant. Margie, age twelve, is the occasional target of remarks made by girls in one friendship group. They call her a nerd because Margie's interest in reading and horses differs from theirs. She gets to know individual girls in this friendship group better through different activities: Mary and she are on the track team together. Joanne and Rika are in her drama class. In each case, meeting the girls apart from school in another activity leads to an enjoyable play date. Word gets around among the friendship group that Margie "isn't so bad."

Margie may not become part of the friendship group, but this will not matter since she has started to form close friendships and neutralized the girls' negative image of her.

The Next Step

You've helped your child get to know other children better because she likes and shares common interests with them. Many children will make the mistake of wanting to be a part of a group even though they don't like the members. If your child selects friends for the wrong reasons, read Chapters Fifteen and Sixteen. If your child is a good judge of potential friends, read Chapters Ten and Twelve to help you plan play dates, and read Chapter Fifteen to help you encourage beneficial friendship choices.

10

Using the Telephone to Make Friends

———•———

The Problem

- My child wants to make his own calls but doesn't understand how to use the phone to get together with potential friends. How can I teach him telephone etiquette?

Background: Developing Best Friends

The best way for your child to make new friends is to have play dates with one other child at a time. Rewarding play dates start with careful planning. As your child gets older, he can take a more active role in planning his play dates. Table 10.1 shows how much you can expect your child to do.

The telephone is a useful tool to help children plan their own play dates and help parents to sharpen their child's conversational skills. When parents monitor their child's phone calls it provides a teachable moment for parents to help children become better conversationalists. When children plan their activities before they get together, they have more fun and fewer arguments.

Conflict between children is the major cause for a play date (and subsequent friendship) to go sour.[1] Much of what children

Table 10.1   Children's Roles in Planning Play Dates

Age	Ways Children Decide to Get Together
Younger than 5 years old	Parents arrange and watch the play date and settle disputes.
5–7 years old	Parents arrange the play date after consulting with child.
8–10 years old	The child makes the call and plans one or two activities with parent's help.
10–12 years old	The child plans the activities; the parents finalize the date and time.

argue about is what activities to do together. This can be avoided by teaching your child to trade information: the playmates then work out together and in advance (not in the heat of the moment) activities they will play.

Seven-year-old Ginny liked to plan play dates in detail. Before Laura came over, Ginny decided that they would first play with dolls and then play dress up. When Laura said she wanted to play jump rope, Ginny got very upset and began to argue with Laura. Neither girl enjoyed this play date.

It was clear that Ginny alone had planned what she and her friend would play. When she learned how to trade information before the play date, she started to include her friend's ideas into their activities. Trading information is done best when the two children talk to each other on the telephone or are alone together waiting at school or an activity. They show each other that they are interested in a play date (and each other) by being interested in talking about common activities. I encourage children to call another child who is a potential play date, with a parent listening to the call. If the child called is rude and is reluctant to talk, then this is a hurtful, although no-nonsense, way of saying that closer friendship is not something she is interested in. If the children can't find a common interest, they will have no idea what to do if they ever get together. In this case, they can end the conversation without an invitation to play.

There are two purposes to teaching your child to trade information. The first is for your child to learn how to share a conversation. A shared conversation is like a Ping-Pong game, with people giving and getting information. Common errors in conversation result in a "conversation hog" (talking only about himself) or an "interviewer" (only finding out about the other person without disclosing any personal information).

The second purpose to teaching your child to trade information is to allow you to teach your child to regulate the level of disclosure in conversations. When people are getting to know each other, their main task is to find out what they like to do together. They stay at a very superficial level and then start to disclose more personal information as they get to know each other better and see if the disclosure is received well and reciprocated. Going too fast in this process may make the other person uncomfortable and less likely to become more intimate.

Solving the Problem: Teach Your Child to Use the Phone to Plan a Play Date

Monitoring a telephone call your child is making to a potential playmate is a great way to have your child learn conversational skills. You put yourself in a key social situation so that you can intervene at a "teachable moment" and yet you won't be noticed by the other child.

Step 1: Teach Your Child How to Leave a Message on an Answering Machine

Answering machines, so necessary for busy people, often confuse younger children. Your child needs to know how to leave a message containing

- His name
- The name of the person he is calling
- His telephone number

Skip this step if your child already knows how to leave a message. If your child doesn't know how to leave a message, here's how to teach him before making a call:

MOM: What would you do if you called Richard but no one was home and the answering machine answered?

PRESTON: I would hang up.

MOM: That would be okay. But it would be better if you left a message. That way he would call you back when he can and you don't have to worry about calling him again. All you have to do is say, "Hi, this is Preston. I'm calling Richard. Call me back at 555-2345." Let's try it. Pretend you're calling Richard and you get the answering machine.

MOM: [Pretending to be on the telephone] *Ring, ring.* "Hello. This is the Jones's residence. We're not available to answer the phone. Please leave a message, and we'll get back to you when we can."

PRESTON: "Hi. This is Preston. Call me at 555-2345."

MOM: That was good! Do you think they'll know you want to talk to Richard?

PRESTON: I don't know.

MOM: Well, let's try it one more time and say you want to talk to Richard.

PRESTON: "Hi. This is Preston. I want to talk to Richard. Call me at 555-2345."

MOM: That was great!

Now that your child is ready to make the call, what does he say? Should he just ask Preston to come over and play? If he does, he is risking a boring and uncomfortable play date if he and Preston don't know what to play. Avoid this by teaching your child to trade information to find out the other child's mutual interests. The goal is to have both children come up with ideas for what to play together. This is also useful practice to build effective listening skills that will help with conversations in general.

Step 2: Practice Trading Information with Your Child

The hardest part about teaching your child to trade information is the "cover story" for the call. He will feel awkward, but almost any way in which he begins asking questions will work. He can ask about homework if the other child is in the same class or how school is going if he hasn't seen the other child in a while. Some children find it helpful to rehearse questions they will ask before they make the call. (Writing these down may encourage getting through the list without listening to the other child.) Before your child makes his first practice call, make a pact that your child needs to find out two things he and the other child would like to play together. Here's how nine-year-old Dennis and his mom practice this just prior to his first call:

MOM: I'd like you to trade information with your cousin Gregory now. I want you to find out two things that you and Gregory would like to play when we get together on Thanksgiving. Let's practice first. Pretend I am Gregory, and you have just called me. "Hello."

DENNIS: What do I say?

MOM: [Whispering] How about, "I wanted to find out what kinds of things you like to play"?

DENNIS: "What kind of things do you like to play?"

MOM: [Pretending she is Gregory] "I like to play basketball. I have a basketball hoop in my backyard." Do you know what else you would ask Gregory?

DENNIS: No.

MOM: Think about the things you like to play that you need someone else to play with. What are they?

DENNIS: Handball, soccer, basketball. Oh, I like to play chess, and I can't find anyone to play with!

MOM: That's a good one, because maybe Gregory likes to play and you could play with him. Let's practice some more. I'm Gregory again. What would you say?

DENNIS: "Do you like to play chess?"

MOM: "Yes. I love it!" That was pretty good! If he doesn't like chess, your job will be to find something he does like.

DENNIS: Okay.

Step 3: Set Rules of Behavior on the Telephone

The errors children most commonly make on the phone are being silly (for instance, making noises on the telephone, having the dog talk, starting the call by saying, "Guess who this is?"), getting too personal, and talking too long. If your child has had a problem staying on the phone too long in the past, agree to a maximum amount of time for the phone call. It is helpful to set up in advance a cover story for why he has to get off the phone—for example, he has to do his homework or has to do chores or what he actually has to do next (see step 6 below).

If your child does silly things on the telephone, add a rule just prior to the phone call:

MOM: I want you to make a good impression with Gregory, so I want you to be serious when you talk to him. Okay?

DENNIS: Okay.

You also want your child to keep from getting too personal and to focus exclusively on finding common activities. This will be easy for most children, but some children may need the help:

MOM: When you talk to Julie, I want you to talk about what you like to do together and not get too personal.

MARY: Can I tell Julie about how much my brother bugs me?

MOM: You don't know Julie that well right now, and talking about that may make her uncomfortable. That's something you should save for when you know Julie better.

Remember, your child is to get information as well as give information. There should be times when he is talking and times when he is listening. If not, then have your child ask an open-ended question (requiring more than a yes or no answer) and wait for the answer. Then repeat the other child's answer and respond to it.

After practicing with you, your child will know how to trade information. Now it's time to make a practice call.

Step 4: Start with a Practice Call

Start your child off with a safe and easy practice call—a cousin the same age as he is will do fine. Have your child find out a few things that his cousin likes to do. Let the other child's parents in on this to make it easier to contact them when you make the call. They may choose to keep your nephew in the dark to make the experience more authentic.

Make these telephone calls private (no one else in the family is to listen in but you). You do this to show your child how important the call is, and he will be more relaxed if you protect his privacy when he eventually calls someone he wants to be better friends with. Make sure there are no distractions and see that he dials correctly and makes the connection. You should hang around when he starts the call to make sure he is following the rules of behavior.

If your child does not want you to stay, leave the room slowly enough to ensure that your child is taking the call seriously. If you hear silliness, immediately remind your child of what he should do. If your child continues to have a problem with silliness, stay close enough to monitor the call and discourage this behavior.

After a couple of these practice calls, your child is ready to use the telephone to plan a play date.

Step 5: Make the Call for the Play Date

Now it's time for the real thing: your child's first call to plan a play date. Help her choose someone she would like to invite, and talk about how they can trade information:

MOM: So you'd like to invite Susan over to play with your board games. What kind of toys does Susan have?

TINA: I don't know.

MOM: I would like you to call Susan and trade information to find out what she would like to play. Find out two toys or games that Susan likes to play with. If you find two, then ask her if she would like to come over and play with those toys. If they are her toys, ask her to bring them. Don't ask her over until you find two toys she wants to play with. I'll listen in and help you if you need it.

Here's an example from a phone conversation between ten-year-old Tammy, an expert at trading information, and her new friend, Linda:

TAMMY: Hi, this is Tammy Gruber. May I speak to Linda?

LINDA: This is Linda.

TAMMY: I just got the latest issue of my teen magazine in the mail.

LINDA: Yeah. Who is on the cover?

TAMMY: J.T.T. Do you want to come over to my house to look at it?

LINDA: Great! I'll bring my magazines.

TAMMY: Great! I hear a dog barking in the background. Is that yours?

LINDA: Yeah.

TAMMY: What kind of dog is it?

LINDA: She's a German shepherd. She's very sweet, and I sleep with her at night.

TAMMY: I love dogs. Does she come up on your bed?

LINDA: Well, my parents allow her only on the floor next to my bed, but when they're not looking, I let her sleep at my feet to keep me warm.

Notice that Tammy is excited to hear from Linda, a sure sign that she wants to be friends. Tammy makes the call easy by trading information to find out about potentially worrisome details. For instance, if Tammy were afraid of dogs, she might hesitate to accept an invitation to Linda's house.

PLAN A

Your child finds two common interests. Until your child has reached her teens, you should arrange play date details with the parents of the other child after the other child accepts the invitation. Get on the phone with the other child's parent, and work out all of the details other than what to play: starting and ending time, transportation, and what meals you are to provide. The more planning and concern you show the other child's parents, the more comfortable they will be with you and your child. It is tempting to let fifth and sixth graders make their own get-togethers. But this is a mistake for three reasons:

1. One child may forget and disappoint the other child.
2. One family may have conflicting plans that the child is unaware of or has forgotten.

3. The guest may not tell his parent where he is and worry
    them.

Ten-year-old Mark excitedly tells his mother that a boy he
asked is going to come over on Sunday to play. His mother is
pleased that Mark can take care of his own social calendar. The
appointed time comes, and the other child doesn't show up. When
his mother calls the other child's parents, they are not aware of
the appointment. Mark is very disappointed.

Here's an example of how ten-year-old Ryan plans his play date
with Darren and then lets his mom take care of the details:

RYAN: What things do you like to play?

DARREN: I like to roller-blade, go biking, and play basketball.

RYAN: Do you like to shoot hoops? I have a basketball net in
my driveway.

DARREN: Yeah, but I'm kind of tired of that. Do you play horse?

RYAN: Yeah. I like that. Do you want to play horse or go
biking?

DARREN: Let's play horse.

RYAN: Okay. My mom wants to talk to your mom.

The moms get into the act now. If Darren had chosen biking,
then the parents would make arrangements for dropping off and
picking up Darren's bicycle and helmet.

Older children trade information in person at school (or use
instant messaging; see Chapter Eleven) instead of on the telephone. Parents still call each other about the final arrangements.

PLAN B

Turn to Plan B if your child doesn't find common interests. If the
other child is not interested in talking or can't agree on what to
play, have your child repeat this step with another child.

Either way, praise your child for trying. I have summarized these steps in the checklist at the end of this chapter.

Step 6: Teach Your Child How to End a Phone Conversation

Until now, you and your child have focused on the beginning and the content of the call. Your child has reaped the rewards of this with well-planned play dates. Now it's time to complete your child's phone etiquette instruction with how to end a call. The opportunity has not occurred for your child thus far because you have gotten on the phone to finalize the play date. If left to her own devices, your child may be abrupt about this. Teach her to wait for a longer pause in the conversation, which means everyone is running out of things to say, and think of a reason to end the conversation in a tactful way—for example: "I have to go now," or "I have to do my homework now." Have your child give one of these cover stories to the other child and say good-bye by saying something like, "I'll see you tomorrow in school." Here's how Mom prepares Samantha:

MOM: Let's pretend you're on the phone with Louise and you are running out of things to say. How can you tell this is happening?

SAMANTHA: I don't know what to say.

MOM: Yes, and if Louise can't also, then you start to hear no one is talking for a while.

SAMANTHA: Oh yeah!

MOM: So what should you do?

SAMANTHA: Get off the phone.

MOM: Yes. How can you do it without hurting Louise's feelings?

SAMANTHA: I don't know.

MOM: Tell her a reason you have to get off, but you probably shouldn't just say you don't have any more to say.

SAMANTHA: Can I say I have to go?

MOM: Yes, because you can't stay on the phone forever. Eventually you have to do things around the house, like go to bed or your homework. You can also say what ever it is you have to do next.

• • •

✓ Checklist for Trading Information ✓

Step 1: Teach your child how to leave a message on an answering machine. Skip this step if your child already knows how. He needs to know to leave

- His name
- The name of the person he is calling
- His telephone number

Step 2: Practice trading information with your child.

- Your child needs to find out two things he and the other child would like to play together.

Step 3: Set rules of behavior on the telephone.

- Take the call seriously—no silly behavior.
- Don't make the call too long.
- Your child should be talking and listening on this call.
- Set up in advance a "cover story" for why he has to get off the phone.

Step 4: Start with a practice call.

- A cousin the same age as he is will do fine.

- Let your relative in on this to make it easier or keep the children in the dark to make the experience more authentic.

- Make these telephone calls private. No one else in the family is to listen in but you.

- Hang around when your child starts the call to make sure he is following the rules of behavior.

- If you hear silliness, immediately remind your child of what he should do. If your child continues to have a problem with silliness, stay close enough to monitor the call and discourage this behavior.

- If your child is doing all of the talking, have her ask an open-ended question, wait and repeat the answer, and respond to the answer.

Step 5: Have your child make the call for the play date.

- Have your child trade information.

- Plan A: If your child finds two common interests, get on the phone with the other child's parent and work out all of the details other than what to play: starting and ending time, transportation, and what meals you are to provide.

- Plan B: If your child doesn't find common interests or the two children can't agree on what to play, have your child repeat this step with another child.

The Next Step

Congratulations! The listening skills you have taught your child will help her throughout her life. She is now ready for the first play date with her newfound friend. The next chapter helps you expand the ways your child can get in touch with friends. Chapter Twelve gives tips for making play dates go well.

11

Using Texting and Instant Messaging to Connect with Friends

———•———

The Problem

- My child's friends use texting and instant messaging (IM) to stay in touch and make plans, and now he wants to do that too. But I have no idea how it works or how to use it to keep track of him during the day.

- I am worried about my child's access to the Internet. What should I do?

Background: New Technology Can Help Friendships

When my son was in fifth grade, IM was relatively new and text messaging was almost nonexistent. I was surprised to learn that many of his friends were using it to communicate with each other on a daily basis (and he wasn't). He had used his computer exclusively to help him with schoolwork. Unlike e-mail, IM from a computer and texting from a cell phone are instant. Many parents provide cell phones to their children for safety reasons—to find out where they are and in case of emergencies. IM can be anonymous, while texting can be traced to a phone (unless it is sent from e-mail). With either IM or text, a child may carry on a conversation with a friend or family without having to reply within a short amount of time and without needing to set time aside to engage in conversation. Older children and teens find texting very useful to the point where studies show that teens prefer texting and IM to talking to the telephone, at least in the United States.[1]

With IM and text, children can keep in constant touch with their friends and family.[2] My son still keeps in touch with friends from high school even though they are in colleges all over the country. When he is on his computer, the buddy list notifies him when a friend comes online and an alarm sounds when a friend sends him a communication. He can decide whether to answer right away or leave it for a convenient break from his work. For parents who are not familiar with IM, here is a typical exchange:

CHESSPLAYER2781 (12:22:02 PM): Hi, did you have trouble with the geography homework?

DANTHEMAN3496 (12:28:12 PM): Yes. But my dad helped me figure it out.

CHESSPLAYER2781 (12:32:27 PM): Wanna go ice skating this weekend?

DANTHEMAN3496 (12:48:32 PM): I can't skate. How about coming over and bringing your bike?

CHESSPLAYER2781 (12:58:32 PM): I just asked my mom and she said OK.

Notice that the exchange takes about thirty-six minutes as each child checks with his parents in order to make plans. In this way, everyone is included in the loop when friends start to make plans for the weekend. Notice that a slow response is common and may indicate that the other person is either busy or is away from the computer.

Since texting originates from a cell phone, children and teens can do it anywhere. However, there is usually a 160-character limit to each message, and most phones don't have a qwerty keyboard, making entering text more difficult. A collection of acronyms has sprouted up that are commonly used for both IM and texting:[3]

Wot u doin 2nit	What are you doing tonight?
Cnt cm out 2 mch	I can't come out, I have too much
hmwk:(	homework + a sad face at the end
B4N	Bye for now

You should become familiar with acronyms such as these:

CD9 or code 9	Parents nearby
MIRL	Meet in real life
P911	Parent emergency
POS	Parents over the shoulder
9	Parent is watching

The following Web site has a list of the top fifty acronyms that parents need to know: http://www.netlingo.com/top50/acronyms-for-parents.php.

Solving the Problem: Help Your Child Set Up His IM Account and Increase Safety Around Internet Use

The steps to take after you have obtained and installed IM software follow.

Step 1: Protect Your Child and Your Computer

Check out spyware blocking and content filtering for inappropriate Web sites to keep inappropriate content from reaching your child and unwanted programs from invading your computer. Some Internet service providers may have their own available. Install and set these up before your child establishes e-mail and IM accounts. There is also software available to let parents monitor incoming calls on their child's mobile phone and caller blocking options on many cell phones. If the child gets a call from someone not on a call list approved by his parents, parents can receive a text alert on their own cell phone or online.

Step 2: Set Up Rules for Computer and Cell Phone Use

Set up your child's computer in a family room, not the child's bedroom. When your child first gets on the computer, help him find interesting kid-friendly sites. Bookmark these, along with your children's favorite sites, so that he can easily return to them. Set specific rules for computer Internet access and cell phone use.

Suggestions for Cell Phone Rules

- Don't download anything that costs money.
- You cannot use the phone during family mealtimes.
- You may have phone contact only with certain people.
- You must maintain your grades to keep your cell phone privileges.
- If someone is bothering or harassing you, don't answer. Tell us. We promise not to take away the cell phone for this reason. (This fear is the main reason children won't tell their parents about harassment.)
- We keep the cell phone at night. (This also helps parents to monitor the calls.)

Some Rules for Computer Use

- Don't give out passwords, addresses, our work numbers, anyone's names or addresses, or the name and location of your school without our okay.
- Don't send your photo.
- Don't download or install software without our okay.

- The Internet is a good place to talk to people you already know but not to meet new people because people may not be who they appear to be online. Someone who claims to be a teenaged girl could be a forty-year-old man. Remember that anything you read online may not be true.

- Never arrange to meet anyone in person you've met online without first asking us.

- Ask us about any offers that involve going to a meeting, having someone visit our house, or sending money or credit card information.

- You do not have to respond to someone or do anything that you don't want to. If someone contacts you online in a way that makes you feel uncomfortable, tell us.

Post these next to the computer and review them before your child gets on the Internet the first time because this is the best time to get her total attention.

Step 3: Help Your Child Choose a Screen Name for IM

Choosing an IM screen name is important because it gives people a sense of identity (not necessarily their own). Tell your child that the name is private and to be given only to other children he likes. It should not identify him in any way. He may have to include a number before or after the name as part of his choice to get the screen name he wants.

Step 4: Teach Your Child IM Etiquette

Internet etiquette is not always obvious. Here are some rules that children should be taught right away so that they make a good first impression:

- Post short messages so others can easily read them.
- Use lowercase. Typing all in caps is like SCREAMING at people.

- Don't use humor or sarcasm; it's hard for others to tell humor and sarcasm in text messages.

- Say good-bye just as you do on a phone call. (Chapter Ten gives tips on how to do this.)

Here's how Dad does this for his fifth-grade daughter:

DAD: Do you know how to talk to your friend on IM?

ANNETTE: Yes. I just type in what I want to say.

DAD: That's right. Go ahead and send a message to Emma.

ANNETTE: [Types a sentence beginning with a capital letter] Like this.

DAD: That's very good. It was a serious sentence. People can't tell if you're joking on IM. It was also short, which is very good on IM. IM is easier than regular typing because you don't usually use any capital letters. So go back and change the first letter. Then send this message to Emma and see what she says back.

ANNETTE: [IMs Emma for about five minutes and then comes back to Dad] I'm finished. What do I do now?

DAD: You say good-bye just like on the telephone. Tell Emma you have to go and you'll see her tomorrow.

These rules can be added later:

- Be kind and friendly to newcomers. They are not sure of what to do and will be a bit unsure of what to say.

- Use the "busy" or "away" feature to tell your buddies when you're going to be away for a long while. Then they won't waste time trying to get in touch with you.

Step 5: Teach Your Child How to Protect Herself

Teach your child about IM blocking. It makes her look offline to people she wants to avoid. If she doesn't want to talk to someone temporarily, she can use the ignore button to block them. This is an effective strategy to use for someone who is being rude.

Step 6: Monitor Your Child's Computer and Cell Phone Use

Get to know her online friends just as you get to know all of her other friends (see Chapter Fifteen). If she surfs the Internet by herself, check her browser history once in a while to see where she's going. You can check up on cell phone calls with the call history. If your child is spending many hours using Internet services, especially late at night, increase your monitoring.

Step 7: Encourage Your Child to Ask for Play Dates Online or by Texting Children They Have Had Play Dates with Before, But You Should Make Final Arrangements

Your child should ask friends over early in the week (even for the weekend) before her friends are busy. She asks you if the day and time are okay. You make certain that her friend's parents approve the play date by following up with a call to them confirming the arrangements.

The Next Step

You have helped your child enter cyberspace in a safe way in order to keep in contact with her friends and continue to get invited to play dates. Thank yourself for providing her with a tool that will help her maintain friendships for many years to come. To learn how to help your child set up rewarding play dates or get-togethers, read the next chapter.

12

Having Fun Play Dates

———•———

The Problem

- How can I make sure that my child has a good time on a play date?
- How can I avoid disasters on play dates?

Background: Obstacles to Rewarding Play Dates

Having one-on-one play dates is the best way for close friendships to develop. Having a play date at your house is your best opportunity to monitor your child's behavior with other children. At their best, play dates provide continuous fun and opportunities for intimacy for both children. Get-togethers (as older children call them) allow older children to confide in each other as their friendship deepens. Furthermore, play dates in your home are better than having children playing in the streets for three reasons: other children may intrude on the play date; others may be watching, and their feelings may be hurt that your child didn't include them; and if your child has been picked on by other children, the bully can try to stop other children from playing with your child. Ideally a child has a better long-term adjustment with two or more best friends (so that he doesn't monopolize a single best friend), and having more best friends doesn't add significantly to long-term adjustment.[1]

The three main obstacles to a rewarding play date are frustration, boredom, and conflict. When you and your child host a play date, you can prevent frustration and boredom through the careful planning I describe in the following steps. I deal with the third obstacle, conflict, in the following chapter.

Solving the Problem: Avoiding Frustration and Boredom on Play Dates

Careful planning will help both children enjoy the play date more. I have grouped the steps by the times at which they are taken:

- Planning the play date (at least a couple of days before it is scheduled)
- Immediately before a play date your child is hosting
- During the play date
- After the play date

Planning the Play Date

Step 1: Decide with Your Child Which Playmate to Invite

Your child needs to select her own playmates with your help.

Seven-year-old Sarah plays with Joanie, her seven-year-old next-door neighbor, two to three times a week. She frequently gets into arguments with Joanie over little things. She is irritable most of the time, especially just after the play dates. Sarah and Joanie's play sessions usually begin when Joanie's mom drops off Joanie for several hours while she does some errands.

Sarah's mom works from her home office, and although Joanie's mom never has offered to take Sarah, Sarah's mom allows this to continue, figuring that at least her daughter has a playmate. But

Sarah's mom has broken the cardinal rule of playmate selection: she never asked Sarah if she wanted to play with Joanie. To her surprise, when she asked, the answer was an emphatic, "No!" Sarah's mom needs to make some important changes.

Sarah's mom politely refuses Joanie's mom's requests for free babysitting. She then begins to invite the children Sarah wants to play with. Within two months, Sarah's play becomes more mature, friendlier, and more cheerful. Her mom is able to get more work done because Sarah needs less supervision when Sarah has a guest over and because Sarah is frequently invited to her friends' houses.

You can also head off similar problems when your child is invited for a play date. Politely handle the invitation while checking with your child. Here's how Andrew's mom does this when Richard's mom calls her:

RICHARD'S MOM: Richard would like to know if Andrew can come over to play tomorrow afternoon after school.

ANDREW'S MOM: Oh! Well, let me check and see if Andrew has any plans. [Asks Andrew out of range of the telephone] Would you like to play with Richard tomorrow afternoon?

PLAN A

If Andrew says he doesn't get along with Richard, the telephone conversation goes this way:

ANDREW'S MOM: It doesn't look like it's going to work tomorrow. Can I call you back when it looks like will work out?

RICHARD'S MOM: Okay.

ANDREW'S MOM: Thanks for calling.

Andrew's refusal can be temporary, and his mom has handled this in a polite way so that she didn't burn any bridges. If Andrew changes his mind about playing with Richard, it is her turn to call and propose a play date.

Sometimes parents misguidedly persist, and it is difficult to turn them down without hurting feelings. Mia is constantly asking for a play date for her four-year-old daughter, Annabel, with Rachel, even though they almost never play together at school and seem to be interested in different things. After politely refusing a couple of times, Rachel's parents finally agree to the play date, and it goes poorly: the children squabble and often try playing without each other. Although Rachel says she wants another play date with Annabel, she doesn't play with Annabel any more frequently at day care after the first play date. Mia continues to ask for play dates. Rather than hurt her feelings, Rachel's mom agrees to a "play date" composed of both children and their parents attending a concert at a local children's museum. When Annabel and Rachel don't play with each other at all, Mia finally gets the message.

PLAN B
If Andrew accepts, Andrew's mom responds:

ANDREW'S MOM: Andrew's free and he would love to. When should I drop him by?

If your child is invited, it is customary for you to offer to drop him off and pick him up.

Step 2: Set Up the Play Date with the Other Child's Parents

Immediately after your child invites another child over (whether it be done by a phone call, texting, or an IM your child has just made, see Chapters Ten and Eleven), get on the phone or speak directly to the other child's parent (you should be doing this until your child is well into middle school). Set up play date times so that you can be there for the entire time. Have your child host play dates only when you can personally supervise. Play dates are too important to leave to others who may not know how to supervise them.

Your job is to set the date and time and to arrange transportation and snacks with the other child's parents. When calling to set up a play date, help set a reasonable length for it.

Joey, age six, is very happy to have Conrad come over to play for the first time. At the beginning of the play date, Joey's mother asks Conrad how long he would like to stay. Conrad says, "All day." Conrad's mother agrees to this, not wishing to offend his newly found friend or Joey's mother. But after two hours, the boys run out of things to play, and Conrad is asking to go home. However, Conrad's mother, who has gone shopping, has turned off her cell phone and cannot be reached. Joey's mother spends the remainder of the play date suggesting activities that the boys don't want to do.

Whether you are the parent of the host or guest, schedule a shorter time than you think the children can manage on the first play date—usually about one to two hours is optimal to start with. A short, successful play date leaves both children wanting more in the future. Ease into longer play dates after several successes. Here's how Conrad's mom does this:

CONRAD'S MOM: [To Joey's mom] When would you like me to pick up Conrad?

CONRAD: I'd like to stay all day!

CONRAD'S MOM: [To Conrad] I know you have been looking forward to playing with Joey, but right now, I need to know what is convenient for Joey's mom.

JOEY'S MOM: You can pick him up in a few hours.

CONRAD'S MOM: How about if I call in an hour and a half and see how things are going?

JOEY'S MOM: That would be fine.

Conrad's mom calls an hour and a half later to find out if the boys are running out of things to do. If they have, she picks up

Conrad. No one is uncomfortable about this arrangement, since the boys have had fun and want to see each other again. The play date is not a burden on Joey's mom, and she has more confidence that her son would be in good hands should Conrad invite Joey for a play date.

Step 3: Make Sure Siblings Are Busy Elsewhere

Siblings have no place in a one-on-one play date. Consider the two following situations.

Seven-year-old Arlene is looking forward to Jane's first visit with her on Saturday afternoon. They decide they will play with Arlene's large collection of toy horses, and Jane brings over some accessories that Arlene does not have. No sooner has Jane arrived than Sam, Arlene's three-year-old brother, becomes interested in the new toys Jane brought. Behaving as a typical three year old, he wants to join in and won't take no for an answer. This upsets Arlene and annoys Jane. Instead of playing by themselves, the girls have to baby-sit for Sam. They never get the special time together each is looking for.

Caroline, age nine, is not looking forward to playing at Samantha's house because Samantha's eleven-year-old brother usually teases them both and destroys their craft projects. The live-in baby-sitter can't control the older brother.

Some parents make the mistake of expecting the older or younger sibling to be included in the play date, or they leave the children to fend for themselves. Although it may stretch a parent's resources, developing a close friendship is important business best done one-on-one without interference. A little extra planning takes care of the sibling and avoids a frustrating experience. Here are some suggestions when you invite a child over for a play date:

- Make your child's room off-limits to siblings during the play date, and strictly enforce this.

- Schedule play dates for siblings at the same time. One at your house and one at another child's house makes it easier for everyone.

- Keep siblings busy with activities that span the play date (for instance, a video). If you can't keep a little brother or sister away for the entire time, schedule a shorter play date.

- Have one parent take the sibling on his or her own special outing while the other parent supervises the play date.

If you have two children close in age, never accept invitations for double play dates where both of your children go to the same house to play with the same child. Each of your children needs to have his own friendships.

Immediately Before a Play Date Your Child Is Hosting

Step 4: Clean Up the Place Where the Children Will Play

Children need a tidy place to play. Usually it's your child's room, the backyard, or a common play area adjacent to an apartment. Children don't like to play in a messy room, even if the mess is their own doing. A parent should pick up the dog poop in the back yard and help a child clean up her room immediately before the play date so these places will stay clean until the play date begins. Here's how Dad gets his daughter to clean up an hour before her play date:

DAD: What did you decide to play with Sheila?

KARIN: We're going to play with my train set.

DAD: There is no clean place to play in your room right now. You need to pick your clothes off the floor and put them in the hamper.

Karin: I'm too tired. You do it.

Dad: I'll help you, but you have to clean up also.

Karin: [Waits for Dad to do it]

Dad: I want you to pick up your underwear, and I will pick up your socks. Let me see you pick up your underwear first. [Karin does this.] I'm sure Sheila is going to have fun playing in this room! [Dad picks up socks.] Now pick up your magazines, and I'll pick up your stickers.

These guidelines will help in cleaning up:

- Allow plenty of time for cleanup.
- Help your child clean up in order to get the process going.
- Don't threaten to take the play date away if your child doesn't want clean her room.

Step 5: Prepare Your Child to Be a Gracious Host

Here are three tips to help you and your child prepare for the guest:

- Have some snacks ready, especially for kindergartners and first graders, to offer when the children get tired of playing. In this way, they have downtime so that the games they were tired of before become interesting again. Older children also appreciate the break and the attention (and it's an easy way to see what they are doing).
- Make noninteractive activities off-limits. Your child doesn't need a guest in your home just to watch TV or play video games (see Chapter Two). It is your job to ensure that your child does not waste a play date by

watching TV or playing video games for most of the time. Also make sure your child doesn't have access to his cell phone.

• Have your child put away any toys he doesn't wish to share or that might be broken. He has to share whatever he leaves out.

During the Play Date

Step 6: Supervise but Don't Include Yourself

When your child is hosting the ideal one-on-one play date or get-together, you are in the background except for an occasional brief chat to get know the other child (see Chapter Fifteen). Your child and his guest need to be in or near your house so that you can hear what's going on. You stay in hearing distance. Be ready to provide a snack, keep siblings away, or step in to resolve disputes that the children can't resolve themselves (see Chapter Thirteen if this is a problem). In other words, you help your child and her guest avoid a frustrating experience.

Your child is totally responsible for the entertainment, so your role is to avoid talking too much to the guest or going on outings.

Ian and Joshua, both eleven years old, are just starting to have get-togethers. On the third get-together, Joshua's father asks them if they would like to go to a movie. They are both excited, and their three hours together consist of driving to and from the movie and watching the movie quietly for two hours. The boys talk to each other for a total of twenty minutes (in the car). They cannot talk about the things they want to because Joshua's dad is constantly asking both of them questions. The result is that they don't get to know each other any better, so this was a wasted opportunity. Ian and Joshua didn't find out whether they liked to play with each other. Joshua's well-meaning father commandeered the play date and gave a lot of his time, but he didn't contribute to his son's friendship.

While your child is building a friendship, avoid movies or other outings with or without parents. These activities are reasonable to do with a well-established close friend, who will feel special being invited along on an occasional outing. However, these will not build a new friendship.

Step 7: Try to Get to Know the Other Child's Parents at Pick Up

Getting to know each other is advantageous for both the guest's and host's parents. Exchanging pleasantries with the other child's parents at the end of each play date shows them that you care about how the play date went and that you are interested in becoming more accessible to them so that setting up future play dates will be easier.

If your child is the guest, be sure that your child thanks the host for having her over. A typical conversation at the end of a play date at Karin's house goes like this:

SHEILA'S MOM: Did everything go okay?

KARIN'S MOM: Very well. Karin had a wonderful time with Sheila. The girls play together nicely. Sheila's such a well-mannered girl.

SHEILA'S MOM: We'll have to have Karin over the next time.

KARIN'S MOM: I'm sure Karin would love that.

Karin's mom compliments Sheila to her mom. Both Sheila and her mom feel appreciated. This will help them feel more comfortable the next time Sheila and Karin play together.

A poor showing is made by the guest's parents if they pull up in front of the host's house to drop off and pick up their child—never getting out of the car. You might have seen these hit-and-run tactics and wonder if the parents have any concern for their child.

After the Play Date

Step 8: Find Out How the Play Date Went

The best way to tell that your child liked playing with the other child is to ask your child in private if he would like to play again with that playmate. Use the answer to guide your future planning for your child's play dates. Don't forget to praise your child for something he did well during the play date.

If your child was the host, stay in earshot so you know what the children are doing. If your child was the guest, ask your child about the play date on the way home. Also ask for details of the play date so that you can judge for yourself. You also want to show your child you are interested in his friends and how he spends his time. Here's a sample conversation between Conrad and his mom:

MOM: Did you have a good time?

CONRAD: Yes.

MOM: What did you do?

CONRAD: Played with Legos.

MOM: What did you make?

CONRAD: I made a fort, and Joey made the cannons.

MOM: What else did you do?

CONRAD: We rode our bikes up the sidewalk.

MOM: Would you like to have another play date with Joey?

CONRAD: Yes!

This sounds like a rewarding play date. Both boys played Legos and rode bicycles together. They didn't just sit and watch TV.

Step 9: Reciprocate Play Date Invitations with Children Your Child Likes

It's considerate and polite for parents to reciprocate play date invitations. You owe this only to parents of children your child likes to play with. If your child has not had fun, don't make or accept another invitation.

When parents reciprocate invitations, each family carries part of the burden for two children getting together. After all, it's a lot of work. Most parents value the children's friendship enough to help in some way. Here are reasonable responses to each of three patterns of exchanging play dates.

PLAN A

If the playmate exchanges invitations, the parents of the guest should immediately offer the next play date at their house. They make a vague statement like, "We'll have to have Joey over to our house." If you are the host, make a vague reply, for instance, "That sounds good. Give us a call." Check with your child in private to confirm he would like to play together, so that you can respond appropriately to a specific invitation.

Exchanging play dates doesn't have to be exactly fifty-fifty. Sometimes the children would rather have it differently.

PLAN B

If the playmate accepts your invitations but doesn't offer his own, you may wonder if you are being used for free babysitting. The worst case is when the other child delays getting back to you and often declines. You wonder if he accepts only when he is desperate. Try not to let this situation continue.

Rest easier if parent and child seem very happy to accept your invitation, they usually accept immediately, and the guest seems delighted to come. In this case, there is probably a reasonable explanation for why the parents are not reciprocating. It may be that both of the child's parents have a full-time out-of-home job. Or perhaps the child comes from a large family, and the parents are too busy scheduling all of the children's activities.

Seven-year-old Allen is very gregarious at school. He always has a smile on his face and is constantly visiting with one group of boys or another. The boys like to play with him. However, after school, Allen must be content to play with his twelve-year-old sister or his fourteen-year-old brother. Allen's parents have put out great effort for the older siblings, who are quite popular. They have friends over constantly and get invited over to óther's houses. But Allen's parents are too busy to take an active role in arranging play dates for him.

If your child likes Allen, he's going to be available and his parents will be grateful. Make sure your child doesn't feel badly that he is not invited to Allen's house. Take the initiative, and don't expect an exchange, although you may eventually get it. Allen's parents will most likely begin to feel guilty about all this work you are doing and will eventually invite your child over.

Plan C

If the playmate turns you down most or all of the time and the family lives far from you, they may be turning you down to avoid driving. In this case, look for children in your neighborhood (see Chapters Four and Five). Avoid inviting a playmate over after he has turned you down twice without offering an invitation to your child.

If the other family never invites your child over but makes play dates with others in your area and if this is happening with many playmates, this can be a polite way of saying that your child doesn't behave well. It's time for a tune-up on the rules of a gracious host in Chapter Thirteen.

• • •

I've given you a lot of hints in this chapter. The checklist that follows helps you put this all together.

✓ Basic Play Date Checklist ✓

Planning the Play Date

Step 1: Decide with your child which playmate to invite.

- Your child is to call and trade information.

Step 2: Set up the play date directly with the other child's parents.

- Host play dates only when you are available to supervise.
- About one to two hours for a play date is optimal as a start.

Step 3: Make sure siblings are busy elsewhere.

- Make your child's room off-limits to siblings during the play date, and strictly enforce this.
- Schedule play dates for siblings at the same time. One at your house and one at another child's house makes it easier on everyone.
- Keep siblings busy with activities that span the play date (for instance, a video). If you can't keep a little brother or sister away for the entire time, schedule a shorter play date.
- Have one parent take the sibling on his or her own special outing while the other parent supervises the play date.

Immediately Before Hosting the Play Date

Step 4: Clean up the place where the children will play.

- Allow plenty of time for cleanup.
- Help your child clean up in order to get the process going.
- Don't threaten to take the play date away if your child doesn't want to clean her room.

Step 5: Prepare your child to be a gracious host.

- Have some snacks ready.
- Make noninteractive activities like the cell phone, TV, or video games off-limits.
- Have your child put away any toys he doesn't wish to share or that might be broken. He has to share whatever he leaves out.

During the Play Date

Step 6: Supervise but don't include yourself. Listen from afar.

- Be ready to offer snacks at a good time.

Step 7: Try to get to know the other child's parents at pick up.

After the Play Date

Step 8: Ask your child in private if he would like to play again with that playmate. Praise your child for something he did well during the play date.

Step 9: Reciprocate play date invitations with children your child likes.

The Next Step

If the play date went well and your child is developing close friendships, then relax: your child is now on the road to having best friends. If the play date was rocky and you frequently had to settle arguments, or the guest doesn't want to get together for a second play date, Chapter Thirteen will show you how to teach your child the rules of a gracious host.

13

Becoming a Better Host

———●———

The Problem

- How can I get my child to be more gracious and engaged when she invites someone over for a play date?
- Can I get my child to argue less and have more fun with his guest?

Background: The Poor Host

Studies show two children will become best friends if they can

- Quickly figure out what to play.
- Avoid or quickly resolve arguments.
- Protect each other's feelings from being hurt.[1]

The poor host finds it hard to agree on what to play, gets into arguments, and doesn't seem to care about his guest's feelings. That's why the poor host finds it hard to make best friends and may be lonely on the school playground.

First graders Katie, the host, and Loren, the guest, are having their first play date. Katie tells Loren the rules (which she makes up) for each game for the whole play date. Loren submissively follows Katie's directions.

Although Katie is excited to have Loren come over to play, she has several major blow-ups. When Loren wins a game or doesn't follow the rules quite to her liking, Katie gets upset and yells at Loren.

At the end of the play date, Loren's mother asks her if she had fun. Loren answers, "No."

Katie's view of a play date is an occasion when she plays the games she wants to play and is the boss. She can do this with her stuffed animals; she doesn't need Loren. Playmates don't want to come back to play with a poor host. After a while, the poor host destroys all her social contacts, leaving no one to invite. Katie needs to learn how to be a gracious host rather than a boss.

I will take you step-by-step through supervising a play date for a child who gets into arguments or is bossy. Through your support and planning, you show your child that play dates are valuable. By staying in the background but stepping in at key times (teachable moments, as some call them) and coaching, you will help your child develop effective social skills and ensure that your child and her guest have fun.

Solving the Problem: Avoiding Conflict on a Play Date

Children who get into frequent conflicts during play dates need help. Start out by having all of your child's play dates in your home where and when you can supervise them. Try to select well-behaved children as your guests. I will show you what to do both before and during these play dates and how to tell if your child is ready to accept invitations from others. I have numbered the additional steps for this play date to be consistent with the step numbers in Chapter Twelve.

Immediately Before the Play Date

Step 4: Put Away Games and Toys That Your Child Doesn't Want to Share

Oddly enough, putting away games and toys that your child doesn't want to share promotes sharing, especially for children between five and nine years old.

James, age six, is very proud of the model ship he put together with this father earlier in the day. When his friend Jeffrey comes over that afternoon, he is eager to show Jeffrey the model. But when Jeffrey wants to look at the model more closely, James yells, "Don't touch!" and gets very angry at Jeffrey for persisting. This is a constant source of friction between James and Jeffrey until Jeffrey loses interest in the model ship.

Imagine that another family invites you to their house at dinner time. They have delicious-looking appetizers attractively set out on platters all over the house, but they don't offer you any (or worse, they forbid you to touch them). It's the same way with a child guest who is shown an enticing toy and is told by the host child that he can't touch.

In addition, there are certain things that your child holds dear. Immediately before the play date, put away the items that your child would not like to share with the guest. Anything your child leaves out for play, he has to share. You do this together with your child:

MOM: Jeffrey is about to come over in fifteen minutes. Are there any toys that you do not want Jeffrey to touch?

JAMES: Can I show Jeffrey the model ship I built this morning?

MOM: If you show him the ship, then you have to let him play with it. Is that all right?

JAMES: No, he'll mess it up!

MOM: Then put it away now. [Mom helps James put it in the closet in her bedroom, along with three other toys James did not want to share. She looks at the toys James leaves out for both boys to play.] Gee, you have some good games here that I know Jeffrey will like to play.

Always prohibit TV, video games, and other noninteractive toys during the play date. If the guest asks for one of these, have your child tell the guest, "My mom doesn't allow me to watch TV or play video games when I have someone over."

Step 5: Review the Rules of a Gracious Host with Your Child

The four rules of a gracious host help children improve their ability to become close friends with others. I will explain each and then show you how to teach them to your child.

• • •

1. *The guest is always right.* This rule neutralizes bossiness and is easy to enforce. If there is an argument—for instance, in the rules of a game or which game to play—the guest is right. You never have to get to the bottom of any argument. Your child needs to learn that a gracious host bends over backward to make a guest feel welcome. A gracious host puts his guest's wishes before his own.

Sometimes the guest is bossy, too pushy, or needs much help. Your child is free not to invite him over again, just as the other child is free not to want to come over again if your child is bossy. The exception is if the guest has physically hurt your child or does not obey you. If the injury isn't accidental or the guest is rowdy and won't obey you, it's time to call the guest's parents for help. If the parent doesn't offer any help, then consider ending the play date and not inviting the guest over again.

2. *If your child is bored, he suggests a change in activity.* Common interests keep a play date going well. Your child has learned how to trade information to find these out before the play date (Chapter Ten). As the children grow to know each other better, the games they have arranged to play will hold their interest throughout the play date. However, the host and his new guest may get tired of playing an activity at different times. Table 13.1 shows three ways that children handle changing an activity when they are bored but their guest is still interested.

Accept only behavior from the "Better" and "Best columns." Younger children will find it easier to suggest an end to the activity ("Better"), while older children are able to make a specific suggestion that the guest will find more interesting ("Best").

Table 13.1   What Your Child Can Say to Change an Activity

Impolite Way	Better Way	Best Way
This is boring.	Can we play something else?	Can we play dominoes when you get one more man out?
I'm tired of playing the mom.	Can you be the mom for a while?	Let's play this for five more minutes and then you'll be the mom. Okay?

3. *Don't criticize the guest.* Again, think of an adult counterpart to this rule. Someone invites you over for dinner and, after a few pleasantries, tells you she doesn't like the way you're dressed and continues to criticize you. I don't think she should be surprised if you never call her or answer her calls. Children also hate to be criticized. Your child should never be impolite. Being

Table 13.2   Polite Ways of Avoiding Conflict

Impolite	Polite
That's a stupid game you picked.	How about we play [name of another game]?
You're cheating.	Can we make a rule that...?
You missed that shot!	Nice try!
My drawing is better than yours.	(say nothing)

polite will eventually get your child what she wants without hurting anyone's feelings. Table 13.2 lists some alternatives. Enforcing this rule means that you will not tolerate jealousy and competition between children.

4. *Be loyal to the guest.* Your child shows that he values the guest when he never invites another child in to play while the guest is still present and never leaves the guest alone for more than a few minutes.

Children are less able to share attention than adults are. If two children are playing together and a third child drops by, not only is the one-on-one play date gone, but three children trying to play together often means that one child gets left out.

Another aspect of loyalty is to stay with the guest throughout the play date. When you find the guest and your child playing in two separate locations, this is due to at least one of the following:

- The two children have failed to agree on what to play next.
- The play date is too long.
- The play date has gone sour: they haven't gotten along well throughout the play date.

• • •

The best time to tell your child the rules of a gracious host is immediately before the guest arrives. List them for your child and have her agree to follow them:

MOM: I want you to remember the rules of a gracious host: You can't play with the toys that we have put away or watch TV or play video games.

MOLLY: Okay.

MOM: Casey gets to pick the games you play.

MOLLY: Okay.

MOM: If you're bored, you can suggest a new game or having a turn if Casey takes too long, but Casey gets to decide.

MOLLY: Okay.

MOM: Another rule of a gracious host is not to criticize Casey.

MOLLY: I never do that.

MOM: Good. I know you won't. Be loyal to your guest—don't leave her alone. Okay?

MOLLY: Okay.

This won't be enough to make your child a gracious host if she never was before, but it will be easier for you to step in, when necessary.

During the Play Date

Step 6: Be Ready to Enforce the Rules of a Gracious Host

Listen from a room close by while doing something you can put down immediately if you have to. Listen to ensure that your child follows the gracious host rules. You are listening for sounds of conflict, forming an impression of the guest, and, of course, thinking about how cute your child is being a gracious host.

Table 13.3 will help you determine how much you will have to step in when your child breaks a rule. You'll find that with every argument, your child has violated a rule of a gracious host. Here are common violations of each gracious host rule:

Argument: You find the children arguing over what toy to play with. The guest is always right.

Rule: The guest is always right.

Argument: The children have been playing the same game for a while. Your child no longer plays in earnest and begins acting silly. The guest gets annoyed by this.

Rule: If they are bored, suggest a change in activity.

Argument: Your child calls the guest names.

Rule: Don't criticize the guest.

Argument: Your child is playing by himself or playing with a child who dropped by unexpectedly.

Rule: Be loyal to the guest.

Show your child that you will not tolerate rule violations. Immediately after each violation, take your child into another room, state the rule clearly, and briefly remind him to follow it. This is the teaching function of this play date, and this is the teachable moment. Having a couple of opportunities for you to teach your child in this way is expected and usually doesn't mar the play date:

TOMMY: [To guest] That's a stupid thing to do! [Referring to a poor move in checkers]

MOM: [From the doorway to Tommy's room] Tommy, I need to talk to you for a minute. Please come here. [Tommy comes.] Thank you. I need to tell you something in the next room. [To the guest] Tommy will be right back.

Table 13.3 Resolving Conflict

Child's Age	What to Expect	How to Handle Arguments
5 year olds	They are poor at sharing and keeping their temper.	You closely supervise their play. They will slowly become better at managing conflict, but don't expect immediate results. When arguments turn into screaming or get physical, immediately give a penalty (step 4) if your child is the offender. Have them jointly apologize (step 5) when they argue for more than a few minutes.
6–7 year olds	Two small arguments during four hours of play is typical. Arguments are verbal only. Children remember and begin to use the rules of a good host.	Enforce the rules of a good host immediately after each argument starts. When arguments turn into screaming or get physical, immediately give a penalty (step 4) if your child is the offender. (Or call the guest's parents and have them talk to the guest.) Have them jointly apologize parents and have them talk to the guest.) Have them jointly apologize (step 5) when they argue for more than a few minutes.
7–8 year olds	Minor arguments once every two or three play dates.	Enforce the rules of a good host immediately after each argument starts.
9–12 year olds	Arguments are extremely rare, mild, and quickly resolved.	Enforce the rules of a good host immediately after each argument starts.

TOMMY: [In the next room] He doesn't know how to play checkers, Mom.

MOM: [Quietly] Remember the rules of a gracious host? [Tommy's silent] Don't criticize who?

TOMMY: The guest.

MOM: That's right. Now what can you say to your guest instead?

TOMMY: I don't know.

MOM: Say nothing when he makes a bad move.

TOMMY: Say nothing?

MOM: That's right. That's the polite thing to do. Try it!

PLAN A

If your child agrees to follow the rule, praise him immediately and allow him to return to his playmate.

PLAN B

If your child disobeys or repeats the same behavior within five minutes, warn your child, and state a clear, immediate, brief penalty—for example:

MOM: If you don't share your dolls with Amanda, you'll have to take a two minute time-out.

MARA: [Starts to share with her guest]

MOM: It's great that you are sharing.

PLAN C

If your child continues to disobey after you've warned her, give her an immediate time-out. Take your child by the hand. Sit her down in a chair or stand her facing a corner away from the guest. Set a timer for two minutes. When it rings, tell your child she can continue playing.

- Don't ask a question when you want your child to obey. ("Don't you think it would be better to share with your guest?" The answer will be, "No!")

- Don't criticize your child. ("You're not being a gracious host.")

- Don't yell at your child.

- Don't lecture your child before or after the time-out.

- Don't send the guest away or threaten to do this—in other words, don't punish the guest!

Giving your child a time-out that she deserves is actually comforting for your child and the guest, since they both learn that you won't tolerate impoliteness. A time-out also ends the argument between host and guest.

Step 6A: Ensure That Your Child Is Loyal to the Guest

If another child comes by or calls, have your child tell him, "I'm busy right now, but thanks. I'll get back to you later."

If you find your child and the guest playing in two different locations, determine the cause before taking action. Ask your child in private if she is having a good time with the other child.

PLAN A

If the answer is yes or the play date has gone well, immediately tell your child to stop what she is doing and join the guest: "Mara, your guest came over to play with you. You need to work out with her things that you will do together."

PLAN B

If the answer is no—she isn't having a good time—and the play date has not gone well so far, it's time for snacks and videos until the other child's parent comes. The play date is technically over.

Step 6B: End Arguments That the Children Can't End Themselves

Five to seven year olds sometimes play too wildly and wind up hurting each other's feelings or sometimes can't end an argument by themselves. They may have trouble moving on past an argument even when they no longer care about the issue they were arguing over. I have heard of older children who gave up on their best friend simply because they couldn't resolve one argument. Children need to learn to resolve arguments quickly and act as if the argument no longer matters to them. Parents can help here.

Six-year-old Dominic, the guest, and Justin, the host, have played very hard during their play date. They start playing with Justin's water pistols and agree that the patio is safe (no one gets squirted). After twenty minutes of play, one boy decides not to honor this and the other boy becomes outraged. Their argument is brief but heated. Neither boy wants to play with the other. They refuse to be in the same room, and Dominic is asking to go home.

Water pistols were a poor choice for the very reason that feelings were more likely to get hurt. You can't use the rule that the guest is always right if the guest has broken the game rules. If the guest does this frequently and it frustrates your child, you can keep the children apart for the remainder of the play date. Your child is free not to invite him over again.

However, Dominic and Justin have been playing well for most of the play date but are in the midst of having a major disagreement. In cases like this, it is helpful for children seven years old and younger to jointly apologize to each other like this:

DAD: It may be time for the play date to end, but I don't want you boys to leave without apologizing to each other.

BOTH BOYS: He's the one who did it, not me. I shouldn't have to apologize.

DAD: I'm not concerned about whose fault it is. You both need to apologize. [Dad looks to see if either boy is willing to start, but both are refusing to look at each other.] Okay, I'm going to count to three. On three, I want you both to say, "I'm sorry." Ready? [He repeats this until both boys are ready.] One, two, three.

BOTH BOYS: [Grudgingly] I'm sorry.

DAD: That's great! [After a minute] Now what do you boys want to do?

JUSTIN: Let's play battleship.

DOMINIC: Okay.

This wouldn't have worked if the boys were still angry with each other or weren't friendship material for each other. Instead, the children quickly changed from sulking to happily playing again. Dad also considers giving the boys a snack after the apology (perhaps they are getting tired and need to take a break from playing) and not allowing them to play with water pistols.

Children over seven years old should be able to end the argument themselves with an apology from one or both. The keys are that they are able to move on without holding the issue against each other and the issues don't come up frequently. If either of these doesn't apply, perhaps they are not friendship material for each other.

After the Play Date

Step 7: Don't Accept Invitations Until Your Child Is Ready

Gracious host play dates in your home help your child develop good habits. Postpone accepting invitations from others until three or four play dates in your home are conflict free. Here are three strategies to politely postpone accepting invitations.

• • •

1. *Try to invite several different children rather than the same child for the gracious host play dates.* Inviting the same child several times is more likely to result in invitations from the other child's parents (eventually what you want, but not before you're sure your child can handle a play date at another's house).

2. *If you want to invite the same child over more than once, do it quickly after the play date.* Call within a day or two of the gracious host play date to set up another for the next weekend.

3. *If your child is invited to another child's house, delay your acceptance:*

Мом: Thanks for inviting Tommy. It would be much more convenient for me to have Jimmy over here again for the time being. Would you mind if Jimmy came over again? I'd be glad to pick him up and drop him off.

• • •

After your child has had three or four successful play dates under your supervision at your home, it is time to accept invitations from others. When you pick up your child after each play date, a simple, "How was he?" or, "Did he listen to you okay?" in a neutral tone of voice opens the door to feedback from the host's parents. Don't say anything to suggest that your child has had a problem. And don't depend on other parents to give you this important information without your asking. They may not tell you if you ask, but they most certainly won't if you don't.

If you find out your child misbehaved as a guest, go back to step 1 before accepting another invitation.

After the play date is over, appreciate the glow from your child. Parents tell me their children ask why other children don't also follow the rules of a gracious host at their houses. There are two answers to poor host behavior of other children. First is to answer:

"When they're at our house, we go by our rules. But I can't make the rules at their house." The second is a solution my son devised for the child who violates the gracious host rule of being loyal to the guest and is illustrated by the following story.

It was not unusual for ten-year old Sol to invite other guests into his house when he was having a friend over for an invited play date. Sol lived on a small street with a lot of other boys living close by, and they would drop in on each other without warning. The last time Benjamin was over, Joe knocked at the door, and Sol let him in. Sol and Joe immediately started playing basketball, a game that Benjamin couldn't play as well. He was consequently left out of the activities for the rest of the play date.

He usually liked playing with Sol and didn't want to give up play dates at Sol's house. So the next time he called Sol for a play date, he asked Sol, "Is there a time we could have a play date when just the two of us could play?" Sol also wanted to keep Benjamin as a friend, so he said yes and made a time. As Benjamin approached Sol's house on this play date, he saw Joe playing with Sol in front of Sol's house. But this time, as soon as Joe saw Benjamin coming, he said good-bye to Sol and left the two of them alone for their play date. Intruders were not a problem for Benjamin and Sol's play dates after this.

You have a lot to put together: the instructions from Chapters Ten, Twelve, and this one. To make it easier, I have combined the information you need into this checklist, with all new instructions marked with an asterisk.

✓ Complete Play Date Checklist ✓

Planning the Play Date

Step 1: Decide with your child which playmate to invite.

- Your child is to call and trade information.

Step 2: Set up the play date directly with the other child's parents.

- Host play dates only when you are available to supervise.
- About one to two hours for a play date is optimal as a start.

Step 3: Make sure siblings are busy elsewhere.

- Make your child's room off-limits to siblings during the play date, and strictly enforce this.
- Schedule play dates for siblings at the same time. One at your house and one at another child's house makes it easier on everyone.
- Keep siblings busy with activities that span the play date (for instance, a video). If you can't keep a little brother or sister away for the entire time, schedule a shorter play date.
- Have one parent take the sibling on his or her own special outing while the other parent supervises the play date.

Immediately Before Hosting the Play Date

Step 4: Clean up the place where the children will play.

- Allow plenty of time for cleanup.
- Help your child clean up in order to get the process going.
- Don't threaten to take the play date away if your child doesn't want to clean her room.

Step 5: Prepare your child to be a gracious host.

- Have some snacks ready.
- Make noninteractive activities like the cell phone, TV, or video games off-limits.

- Have your child put away any toys he doesn't wish to share or that might be broken. He has to share whatever he leaves out.

- *Briefly review the rules of a gracious host:
  1. The guest is always right.
  2. If your child is bored, he suggests a change in activity.
  3. Don't criticize the guest.
  4. Be loyal to the guest.

During the Play Date

Step 6: Supervise, but don't include yourself. Listen from afar.

- Be ready to offer snacks at a good time.
- *Be ready to enforce the rules of a gracious host immediately after each violation.
    - *Take your child into another room.
    - *State the rule clearly and briefly remind him to follow it.

    *Plan A: If your child agrees to follow the rule, praise him immediately and allow him to return to his playmate.

    *Plan B: If your child disobeys or repeats the same behavior within five minutes, warn your child: State a clear, immediate, brief penalty.

    *Plan C: If your child continues to disobey after you've warned her, give her the penalty you warned her about immediately.

*Step 6A: Ensure that your child is loyal to his guest.

*Step 6B: End arguments that the children can't end themselves.

Step 7: Try to get to know the other child's parents at pick up.

After the Play Date

Step 8: Ask your child in private if he would like to play again with that playmate. Praise your child for something he did well during the play date.

Step 9: *Don't accept invitations until your child is ready.

- Reciprocate play date invitations with children your child likes.

The Next Step

You and your child have had the experience of a well-planned and smoothly running play date. Your child will start getting closer to children she frequently sees on play dates, and you will also come to know these other children better. The next chapter looks at how to help your child make and keep friendships over vacations. Chapters Fourteen and Fifteen help you to teach your child how to make wise choices for close friends.

14

School Break and Vacation Activities That Promote Friendships

———————●———————

The Problem

- Over vacations, my son seems lonely and gets addicted to video games. What should I do?
- Over vacations, my daughter loses touch with her friends. What should I do?
- What kind of camp experience would be best for my child?

Background: Making the Most Out of Vacations

School vacations present unique problems for you and your child. If both parents are working, you have to make arrangements to have your children supervised. If one parent stays home, it is still better to structure the day so that your children don't turn into starchy vegetables in front of the TV or video game console. Ideal vacation activities, from the perspective of promoting friendships, are ones that

- Have adequate adult supervision and planned activities.
- Draw other children from your neighborhood.

- Promote a large amount of physical activity.

- Expose your child to new activities that many other children like to do, thus expanding interests he may have in common with other children.

However, if your child has difficulty meeting new playmates, read Chapter Seven first. If your child has difficulty being a good sport, read Chapter Eight first. If your child is well-behaved, here are alternatives you might consider.

Day Camps

Day camps hold three advantages for children and their parents. They can organize the bulk of the day for children for several weeks of vacation. They can encourage children to try new activities that might later pan out to attract friends. And they can help your child find new friends who will be easy to get together with on a continuing basis even if these children attend a different school than your child does.

Price is generally not related to quality in day camps. Nonprofit camps are typically less expensive than private camps. Cub Scouts sometimes run day camps, which focus on scouting activities. They are relatively inexpensive because they are staffed with volunteers. We were fortunate to have a sea camp in our area that taught Boy Scouts how to sail. Older scouts, who had been through it before, were put in charge of instructing younger scouts, so they learned a little about leadership.

Day camps are either specialized, single-activity programs (golf, music, art, dance, science, music, or horseback riding) or more general. Perhaps the most useful, in my opinion, are sports camps. I like them because they promote exercise in a social context. Many adults who manage to work out regularly will tell you that exercising in a social context is much easier and more fun to do regularly than exercising alone.

Parents frequently tell me their child is "not a sports person." However, I find that when children are given the opportunity to play and have fun, they become more comfortable with sports.

If your child is really interested in the activity, he can meet others with a similar interest. Your child will listen more attentively to an adult coach and learn more than from you trying to teach him. If the camp groups children together by sports ability, this will ensure that he will have fun. Multisports camps can expose young children to a wide variety of activities, so that they find sports they can play well enough to play with others.

One summer, eleven-year-old Simon's parents enrolled him in golf camp. The reason that they selected golf camp was that two of Simon's friends were enrolling in the camp at the same time; if he didn't participate, he wouldn't be able to have get-togethers with them during the day anyway.

Simon had never played golf before and protested bitterly, but his parents made him go for two days to give it a fair try. They said if he didn't like it, he could stop then. At the end of the second day, he wanted to continue. By the end of this first week, his enthusiasm was so infectious that his dad (who disdained golf himself) had him teach what he had learned. It helped bring Simon and his dad together and gave them something to talk about besides the usual parental pestering. He continued to have get-togethers with the friends who also enrolled and he now had one more interest in common with them.

Sleepover Camps

If one of your goals for a vacation activity is to promote friendships for your child, sleepover camps are riddled with disadvantages: they are usually the most expensive alternative, they draw children from a wide geographical area so that forming a lasting friendship is unlikely, and they interfere with ongoing friendships unless the friends come with them to camp. If your child has difficulty with group situations (typically children are in groups of ten at sleep-away camps), you may not find out things are going poorly until it's too late.

Sleepover camps sponsored by scouting or religious organizations or other nonprofit organizations may be less expensive than private camps and may draw on the child's existing peer group, thus overcoming two disadvantages of this type of camp. For instance, if your child has many friends in his or her scout troop (or religious youth group), then this would be a reasonable, low-cost sleepover experience. Parents can monitor their child by coming along on a couple of weekend campouts before committing to the sleep-away experience. Many troops encourage parents to come along on the summer camp to help out with supervision. The disadvantage to scout camps is that they usually are only one to two weeks long and do not span a whole summer vacation.

Camps for Children with Special Needs

It is rare to find vacation activities, even at the higher prices, with adequate supervision to handle children with special needs. If children give camp counselors problems, they usually just ask the child to leave the camp. Some children constantly draw negative attention to themselves, and before long they become targets of both counselors and peers. Camp is not a worthwhile experience under these circumstances unless the counselors are trained appropriately. Camps for special needs children can (but not always) have trained staff who better understand and know how to deal with the children's problems.

You have to apply early for camps for children with special needs (usually around March for the following summer) because they have limited space and quickly fill up. The major disadvantages to camps for children with special needs are that they may group children together who would not make suitable friends for each other, they can be far away from you (and unlikely to promote lasting friendships), and they are expensive.

Children with attention-deficit/hyperactivity disorder or conduct problems are better off not being friends with each other. This doesn't necessarily apply to well-behaved children with developmental disabilities or high-functioning autism spectrum disorders. These children may feel more accepted when they are grouped with other children at the same social and cognitive levels of functioning and interests.

Enrolling your child in a camp experience has an element of risk. The camp requires payment in advance but may be at least partly nonrefundable. And there is no guarantee that you will get your child to attend. The next section offers my ideas for dealing with this risk.

Solving the Problem: Getting Your Child to Try a Day Camp

I have identified the major issues with camps. Becoming familiar with these puts you in a better position to avoid the pitfalls.

Step 1: Choose an Activity That Will Benefit Your Child

This is done well in advance of the vacation—perhaps three or four months before school is out for the summer. Many children may be agreeable at this point but balk when the time comes to go to camp. You may have to get behind your choice when the time comes, so it is better for you to have a well-thought-out rationale for why this experience will be beneficial to your child. It will be something you can tell your child to get her to go, and tell yourself in case there is resistance, and you will be more likely to have the resolve to persist.

If your child has trouble listening to adults or has other special needs, the special needs camp may be your best alternative. Beginning sports camps are beneficial for children who need more exercise or need to branch out in interests. Ask about how groups are organized, how experienced counselors are, and how the camp handles discipline. Consult with the parents of your child's friends to see what camps they are considering. If parents work together in this way, it will ensure that children will be more likely to want to go to camp when the time comes.

Step 2: Plan Vacation Play Dates Ahead of Time

Children will be more willing to attend camp when the experience has minimal impact on play dates with their favorite friends. Scheduling play dates in advance is the most beneficial way to deal with the vacation anyway. Before the start of the vacation, call the parents of all your child's regular playmates in order to make up a vacation calendar listing when each friend is going to be out of town. Many parents will be eager to work out a vacation play date schedule to ensure their children play together while both children are in town.

Step 3: Make the First Two Visits to Day Camp Mandatory; Then Let Your Child Choose to Continue

Your first priority is to get your child to give the camp a try. Make it mandatory that he go at least twice (unless you have no choice but to send him because you have no place else to put him while you are at work), so that he can make an informed choice. Ten-year-old James doesn't want to try the sports camp his mom enrolled him in a few months ago:

MOM: Sports camp starts next week. You will need some new shoes, so let's go to the shoe store.

JAMES: I don't want to go. I just want to stay home.

MOM: You will get bored if you stay home with nothing to do. You need to give sports camp a try to see if you would like it. Your friend Sal is going. You won't be able to play with him during the day when he's at camp anyway, so you might as well go.

JAMES: But I don't think I'll like it.

MOM: I want you to try it for at least two times. If you don't like it after the second time, then we can stop if you want.

PLAN A
James agrees.

PLAN B
James doesn't agree or balks the night before camp. Sometimes children are fearful of new experiences. It may be helpful to offer a small reward for going the two times: all James has to do is attend, and he will get a game he likes. Parents can also explain in more detail what the first day might be like to calm James's worries.

JAMES: I don't want to go. I think it will be lame.

MOM: Your dad and I think you need to try it. It won't be so bad. They have a schedule each day of different sports they do for about an hour and a half each. If you don't like a sport, it won't last that long—certainly much shorter than being bored all day at home. I'm not going to let you stay home and watch TV all day. Also Sal isn't that interested in sports, and he's going to try them out.

JAMES: I still don't want to go.

MOM: We only want you to try it out. So you only have to attend Monday and Tuesday. If you go both days, we'll get you that video game you like.

Step 4: At the End of Each Day of Camp, Ask Your Child Whom He Played With

Find out which children your child plays with at day camp. Focus on those who live in your neighborhood, and add these children to your child's play date invitation list. In this way, you take lasting advantage of the camp experience and also ensure your child will continue to want to go to the camp.

The Next Step

School breaks and vacations may be no vacation for parents, but with careful planning and the right choice of activities, school vacations can be important and enriching experiences for children. Read Chapter Six for tips on how to turn friends discovered at camp into play dates.

PART THREE

Keeping Friends

If you learn how to listen to your child, she will confide in you, and you will be able to help her with her problems. Become a better listener, and she just might listen to you when you guide her in her choice of friends.

15

Encouraging Wise Choices

———————●———————

The Problem

- How can I get to know my son's choices for friends without appearing intrusive and meddling?
- I don't know what kind of children my daughter's friends are. How do I learn more about them?

Background: Encouraging Beneficial Friendship Choices

I will never forget the first time I visited Mark Siedler's house. I was thirteen years old, and Mark was to become one of my closest friends for many years. I walked in his front door with him, expecting to say a perfunctory hello to his mother and then go off to his room with him. This was standard operating procedure with every other new friend I had made. Boy, was I wrong! I found myself sitting with his mom, having an uncomfortable, but meaningful conversation.

She was giving me the third degree—putting me on the spot about my interests and aspirations. I was uncomfortable because no parent had ever before asked me so many personal questions.

Yes, I wanted to go to college. Yes, I was looking forward to school. Yes, I was interested in girls but wasn't dating anyone. As my armpits were getting soaked from perspiration, Mark was calmly sitting next to me.

There was a short silence, and Mark took me to his room. I was acceptable to his mom, and in passing this test, I felt really good about myself. Mark was waiting and watching throughout all of this. When his mom finished, he smiled at me and took me up to his room. Mark overheard a lot about me, and when we went to his room, we continued speaking as if we had started our intimate conversation. I had a lot of respect for Mark's mom after that and wished I could talk to my own parents the same way.

Like Mark's mom, you can guide your child to choose friends wisely. Start this now, rather than waiting until your child is an adolescent. You do this in three ways:

1. Let your child know you consider her friends to be important people.
2. Encourage your child when she makes wise choices.
3. Discourage her from seeing children who are poor choices as friends.

This chapter deals with the first two ways you help your child. These are ways that boost your child's self-esteem. Following the steps in this chapter will make it easier for you to follow the steps in the next chapter to discourage friendships you do not like.

Solving the Problem: Support Your Child's Wise Friendship Choices

You influence your child's choice of friends by helping your child select whom to invite for play dates.

Step 1: Talk to Your Child's Friends, Especially the First Time They Come Over

The third degree I got from Mark Siedler's mom was a practice Mrs. Siedler had started very early in Mark's life. Now is the time for you to know your child's friends better. Prepare a snack, and plan on briefly joining your child and his guest during an occasional play date. Treat the guest respectfully as a child his age. Your goal is to get the guest to talk about his interests and values:

- Start with an interest your child has told you about.
- Be serious but warm.
- Be friendly, but maintain an adult distance.
- Keep conversations short—ten minutes is enough—so that your child can continue with his play date.

Here's a sample conversation between Kelsey's mom and Vicki, age nine, Kelsey's new friend:

MOM: Kelsey tells me that you're doing your school science project on crystals.

VICKI: Yes. I'm getting crystals to grow in a jar on my window sill.

MOM: How did you pick crystals for your project?

VICKI: I like the way they look after they're grown. They look like little jewels.

MOM: Is anyone helping you grow them?

VICKI: My dad. He also showed me how to make a poster on our home computer so I can display my project.

Kelsey's mom discovered a lot about Vicki in this brief conversation: her family's attitude toward school, that her dad is involved with helping her, and that Vicki is not a child who puts off things until the last minute. If Kelsey values school work, it is important for her to choose friends who feel the same way. This is so that they will understand Kelsey's concerns about school, will not distract her from her goals, and will give her emotional support with school issues.

Studies show that many girls' self-esteem starts to decline in junior high school.[1] Prevent this decline by helping your daughter choose as friends other girls who will support her and help her feel good about herself and her interests.

Step 2: Talk to Your Child About Other Children's Reputations

Learning about the reputations of your child's acquaintances will help you make informed decisions about them. The best source of information is your child. Learn more about the friendship groups in your child's grade. Talk to your child about who gets in trouble, who excludes other children, and who bothers other children when they are playing. Here's a conversation between a dad and his eight-year-old son as they are driving to school in the morning:

DAD: What does your school monitor do when someone does something bad or breaks the rules?

SAM: They get benched [sit on a designated bench for a few minutes] or write standards [a countereducational practice of using a boring writing assignment as punishment, confusing penmanship with punishment].

DAD: Does anybody get benched or write standards?

SAM: Danny gets benched at every recess.

DAD: What does he do to get benched?

SAM: He hits other kids.

Here's a similar conversation between a mom and her fifth-grade daughter:

Mom: Who are Jeanette's friends?

Heidi: Wendy, Jessica, and Vanessa.

Mom: What do they talk about?

Heidi: Boys and clothes.

Mom: Are they interested in sports?

Heidi: No. That's more Cynthia, Diane, and Liz. They play soccer.

Mom: Who does Ann hang around with?

Heidi: I don't know. Most of the girls don't like her. But she has some friends.

Mom: What does she do that they don't like?

Heidi: She's kind of bossy.

You'll be surprised at how interested your child will be in this conversation. Learn the names of the other children in the class who are the same sex as your child, and keep informed by having short discussions like the one above every few weeks. You are giving your child the message that he should avoid children with a negative reputation and that other children's interests are important to know.

There are two guidelines for these sorts of conversations:

- Don't assume that another child's reputation is permanent. Sometimes children like Ann shape up and become better behaved.

- Don't ask about popularity, since you would be calling attention to this as a factor in choosing friends. (See the next chapter to find out why to avoid discussing popularity.)

Step 3: Praise Your Child for Wise Friendship Choices

Praise your child by speaking warmly about her and her friend. This is best done in private, during a quiet time, as soon after the play date as convenient:

MOM: [As they watch Vicki's mom driving away with Vicki in the car] Vicki has a good attitude about school. Do you like her?

KELSEY: Yes.

MOM: She seems like a nice girl.

The Next Step

You have shown your child you are interested in her friends. This is sure to bolster her self-esteem and your relationship with your child even when she is a teen. You also gain the credibility to advise her on poor choices. The next chapter shows you how to do this.

16

Discouraging Poor Choices

———●———

The Problem

- My son wants to be friends with a crowd I don't like. What can I do about it?

- How do I help my child make better choices in friends?

Background: Five Common Types of Relationships for Your Child to Avoid

When children are younger than twelve, parents can have a great influence on selecting the children with whom they become friends. The focus of this chapter is on helping your child select friends based on protecting his self-esteem, as in the first two examples, and providing positive social influences, as in the last three examples.

The Popular Child Trap

Your child should select friends because he likes them and they're available, not because they're popular. Here are two examples of what can happen when your child falls into the popular child trap.

Allison wants to invite a boy for her ten-year-old son Steven to play with, hoping to expand Steven's friendship group. She asks Steven whom he wants to invite. Steven picks Frank, one of the most "popular" boys in his class. In fact, Frank is the only one he wants to invite. Allison tries three times over the next two weeks to invite Frank. Although Frank's mother never says no, she can't come up with a time when he is available. Finally, Allison gives up, and Steven is heartbroken.

Reena invited Tai, the most popular girl in her class, to her eleven-year-old birthday party even though they had barely played together before this. She was flattered that Tai agreed to come. Although there were lots of activities and a delicious cake, Tai looked as if she would rather be somewhere else. She opened her party favor, a paint-by-numbers set, and played with it by herself for the remainder of the party. The next day at school, Tai told the other girls how boring Reena's party was.

Many children looking for friends select a very popular child who is too busy with friends he already has to make new ones. Avoid setting your child up for disappointment by asking these questions:

- Is the child nice? Studies show that how children rate popularity is determined to a high degree by attractiveness, size, strength, and physical ability. The most popular children are not necessarily the nicest.[1]
- Will the child be able to get together with your child reliably enough for a meaningful friendship to develop? A popular child may work your child into his busy schedule once a month or less.

One-Sided Friendships

In a one-sided friendship, one child takes advantage of the other without offering anything in return. Here are some examples of one-sided friendships to discourage:

- Twelve-year-old Susan visits Diane just to swim in her pool. When the pool is being repaired, Susan avoids Diane at school.

- Eleven-year-old George is afraid to say no when Jerry wants to copy his school work for fear that Jerry will not let him hang out with him.

- Eight-year-old Bradley likes to go over to Miles's house because Miles has neat video games. But Bradley does not like to hang around with him at school and doesn't invite him over to his house.

One-sided friendships are not beneficial for either child. They take away time from playmates who will really like each other.

Poorly Behaved Children

In a regular elementary school class, the chances are that about 10 percent of the children (three or four out of thirty students, mostly boys) will draw attention to themselves with poor behavior.[2] Six-year-old Scott, for example, wants to invite Rodney over. The two boys know each other well from school, since they are both frequently benched together by the teacher for misbehavior. Both Scott's and Rodney's parents discourage this friendship until both children behave better at school. In this way, parents give the clear message, "We don't want you to hang around with kids who get into trouble."

A child looking for friends may select a child with a negative reputation out of desperation or because the other child approaches him and he is flattered by the attention. Parents of friendless children tell me they go along with this choice: "Who else is my child going to play with?" My answer is, "It's better to wait for the right friends than to have your child run with the wrong crowd." A child who listens to the teacher and gets along with classmates makes a better playmate for these reasons:

- He has more to teach your child about consideration for others.

- He is unlikely to have a negative reputation, so that your child will not be guilty by association with him in school or elsewhere.

- He will be less likely to break rules in your house and will make play dates easier for you to supervise. You and your child will both look forward to him coming over.

Children with Poor Values or Antisocial Interests

Children seek out others like themselves and become more like the others they associate with.[3] Thus, it is critical for parents to be aware of their children's associates and act proactively to ensure that those associates are a positive influence.

Candace is an intelligent and well-read fourth grader whose parents don't want to rush her into being interested in boys. She, however, desperately wants to join a friendship group of popular girls who are interested in boys, clothes, and makeup but don't value doing well in school. Despite play dates with two of the girls in this circle, the other girls continue to snub her. Meanwhile, she has avoided getting together with Barbara, although Barbara and she have several interests in common, like reading and cooking.

The girls Candace is trying to befriend do not value her strengths and reject her for her looks. Candace is doing the same thing to Barbara. Barbara and Candace may not hit it off, but how is Candace to know unless she tries?

As another example, fourth graders Jay and Julian are great friends who share a favorite activity of picking on Fred. Whenever they meet Fred, they threaten him. One day when they are riding their bicycles home from school, they get on both sides of Fred, box him in, and threaten to break the spokes of his bicycle. Jay and Julian are great friends because of a mutual antisocial interest: bullying poor Fred. If their parents allow this friendship to continue, they may be headed into worse trouble as they get older.[4]

Children with Behavioral Problems

Studies show that two children with conduct or behavioral problems are better off not being friends with each other.[5] Parents are often tempted to get children like this together because they are using the same services or appear to have the same temperament (that is, they have something in common). This is a mistake. These children tend to become much more poorly behaved when around each other and exacerbate each other's negative reputations. When asked in private, they rate the friendship with the other child with behavioral problems as of poorer quality than friendships with more typically developing children.[6]

The research is clear that children with behavioral problems and conduct disorders are better off not being friends with each other. However, no such research exists for children with Asperger's disorder, mild autism, and social communication disorders. My preference (until I am better informed by research studies) is to give children with these disorders a chance to associate with typically developing children. Parents should evaluate if these friendships are beneficial. Do the children feel comfortable with each other and accept and support each other? Does their relationship promote more mature behavior?

Solving the Problem: Discouraging Poor Friendship Choices

Step 1: Start by Giving Your Child the Reason That the Friendship Is Not a Good Idea

If your child is taking advantage of another, explain why the other child's feelings are important. Keep the explanation simple:

MOM: Why do you like to go to Diane's house and play?

SUSAN: I like to swim in her pool.

MOM: Is that the only reason?

SUSAN: I don't know.

MOM: Do you like Diane?

SUSAN: She's kind of a nerd.

MOM: It's wrong to do that to Diane, because she thinks you like her. It's not fair to her, and you will probably have more fun playing with someone you really like.

It will be difficult for you to know if some of your child's friends are poor choices unless you have gotten to know them or you know why your child wants to play with them. (Read Chapter Fifteen to learn how to encourage wise friendship choices.) Following the steps in the previous chapter will also give you more credibility with your child, so that she will be more likely to listen to you when you want her to stop playing with a poor choice. When you listen in on play dates, you will have specific examples to give your child as reasons for discouraging these friendships; usually they are related to the other child being a poor guest. Here the reason for the poor friendship choice is based on what the other child does. Focus on this in your explanation:

MOM: I know you would like to have Sean over because he wants to play with you so much. Do you have fun playing with him?

PAUL: I don't sometimes, but he likes me!

MOM: I know he does, but it's very hard for me to have him over because he isn't nice to you and he doesn't listen to me.

Step 2: Make a Pact with Your Child About a Playmate You Do Not Like

Make a temporary compromise with your child: you agree to allow your child to play with the playmate you don't like if your child agrees to play with others you both like first.

Your strategy is to give the child who is a better choice a chance at your house and to help your child see the difference between poor and better choices. Limit the damage if the child is hard for you to manage or is rude or unkind to your child. One way to limit the damage is to put a price on play dates with poor choices (see the exception below). Here are some ways to limit the damage.

PLAN A

If your child has several acquaintances but her first choice is a poor choice, have her pick her second choice (one you also like). When she has a play date with choice 2, that child may become choice 1, and the other child will be forgotten. It may be necessary for you to make a pact with your child. In this case, I advise not sharing your reasons for not wanting to invite the poor choice for the following reasons:

- Not allowing your child to play with the poor choice in your home may have the opposite effect in school. It makes some children more likely to play with the poor choice.
- Your child may share your stated preferences with the child who is the poor choice. If you wind up living up to your pact and inviting this child to your house, he may be even more poorly behaved if he knows you don't like him.

Here is an example for this situation:

MOM: I'll make a deal with you. First you invite over two other children. Then if you still want to, you can invite over Sean.

Always offer to live up to your end of this deal. Invite Sean over. The play dates don't have to be the same length. For example, the two children you like each stay for three hours, but Sean stays for an hour and a half. Here's what Mom says before she lets her son invite Sean:

MOM: Okay, I've agreed to let you invite Sean over. We'll invite him for an hour and a half.

Neither you nor your child has to put up with hurtful or disrespectful behavior from the guest. If the guest does not obey you, call his parents and have them either come up with a way he will obey you or make arrangements to end the play date early.

PLAN B

If your child has no choice in playmates but a poor one, make a pact:

MOM: First try to meet other children in the park or at school [see Chapter Seven before you do this with your child]. Then if you still want to, you can invite over Sean.

Always offer to follow through with a play date with a child you think is a poor choice if your child completes his part of the deal. But there is an exception: cut off contact with a friend your child gets into trouble with. In this case, say to your child:

DAD: I'm sorry. I can't allow you to play with Rodney. You have both been in serious trouble together, and you have lost your freedom to get together with each other.

Step 3: Be Firm About a Poor Choice for a Playmate

Even if your child still likes a playmate you consider a poor choice, you do not have to put up with a child who doesn't listen to you. Tell your child why you don't want to invite him over again:

MOM: I know you like to play with Sean, but he's too hard for me to take care of. I cannot invite him over again until he's able to behave himself better.

The Next Step

You now know when and how to discourage poor friendship choices. Help your child replace them with children who make better friends. Now you can start working together with your child to promote close friendships with children you both like. If your child has few children to choose from, read Chapters Four and Five. Chapters Ten and Twelve will help you and your child plan play dates. Review Chapter Fifteen in order to support your child's wise friendship choices.

17

Listening to Your Child's Worries

———●———

The Problem

- My child doesn't talk to me about his social life. How can I get him to tell me more?

- I sense that my child is having some problems with her friends. What should I do?

Background: Finding Out About Your Child's Social Life

I feel lucky that my son wanted to talk to me about things that bothered him when he was in elementary school. It had been hard for me to talk with my parents. I was afraid of what they might say or do and couldn't imagine that they could understand my problems. As an adult, I now realize that I would have been a lot less worried as a child if I had spoken to them about things that bothered me.

You won't be able to help your child with his problems unless you know what they are. The next steps will help you to get your child to talk to you about problems.

Solving the Problem: Listening to Your Child's Problems

Your child will talk to you more if he feels you are an attentive listener, won't try to help him solve problems before you have heard enough to understand what they are, and wait for him to ask you for advice. He will more naturally turn to you for help. Like other things you've learned to do effectively as a parent, your patience will be rewarded.

Step 1: Try the Direct Approach First

I'm sure you've already tried the direct approach to get your child to talk to you. Here are some hints to make it work better.

- *Better times:* When there are no pressures and you are alone with your child and relaxed—for example:
  - When walking with or driving your child from school. Don't play the radio if you're in the car. Leave earlier to get to school, and on the way home after school, walk more slowly with your child than you usually do.
  - When playing a simple game requiring little concentration. Be prepared for lots of breaks in the conversation.
  - While eating together with your child and no one else is at the table.
  - A few minutes prior to bedtime.
- *Body language:* Move closer to him. Allow your child to move away if he doesn't want to talk, but wait a few seconds to see if he comes back.
- *Eye contact:* Girls: Look your daughter in the eye. Boys: Walk or sit side-by-side, glancing at your son's eyes once in a while.

- *Voice tone:* Clearly audible and empathic. Avoid humor or smiling.
- *Opening line:* Make it short but to the point:

  "Tell me about your day."

  "You look as if you've had a hard day at school. Want to talk about it?"

  "Were you able to patch things up with Kayla?" (Dad knows that his daughter has had a falling out with Kayla.)

If your child doesn't want to talk, don't keep asking questions. Instead open the door to talking about it later:

DAD: Is anything bothering you?

ANN: [Obviously agitated] Nothing.

DAD: Oh. It seems like something is bothering you. Maybe I'm wrong, then.

Your child may not talk to you when you ask, but she may when you least expect it.

Talk with your child in a matter-of-fact way. Rephrase what your child is saying in a neutral tone of voice; ask questions related to who, what, and where; and get all the details you can before asking for reasons:

ANN: The girls have been avoiding me at school.

DAD: They've been avoiding you?

ANN: Yes, when I go over to sit with them at lunch, Amy tells them to move.

DAD: What happens next?

ANN: They all move to another table and leave me sitting alone.

DAD: Is this the first time they've done this to you?

Be patient. Let your child talk about her problem as slowly as she wants. Avoid the following mistakes, which will stop your child from talking or make her feel brushed off:

- Trying to solve the problem before your child is through describing it

- Showing your child you're upset (even if you are)

- Criticizing your child or her friends in any way .

Step 2: Be Prepared to Find Out Later

If your child isn't ready to talk when you want to listen (or begins to talk but doesn't want to continue), be ready to listen when he wants to talk. My child would talk about things that were bothering him before he went to sleep. I'd be tired and looking forward to getting things done around the house, when all of a sudden he'd get chatty. I know that he was less defensive at bedtime. Things he put out of his mind during the day had a nasty habit of creeping up late at night. So this was my chance to find out if I was receptive. Here's how a scenario between nine-year-old Alisa and her mother begins:

MOM: Time to go to sleep now.

ALISA: I'm not tired.

MOM: Try to get to sleep.

ALISA: [As mom is leaving her bedroom—I usually found the conversation beginning just as I was on the way out my child's bedroom door] Cory said that if I don't give her my lunch money, she won't be my friend.

MOM: [Comes back and sits on her bed] What did you do when she said that?

ALISA: I didn't give it to her. She said she wouldn't be my friend anymore.

MOM: What do you think about that?

ALISA: If she won't be my friend because I didn't give her money, I don't think she's that good of a friend.

MOM: I think you're right.

Mom asks Alisa what she thinks. This gives Alisa a chance to think through what is going on. Then Mom can give her the credit for solving her own problem. If Alisa chose unwisely, Mom would ask a question like, "What makes you say that?" in order to help Alisa think through the problem better. She then helps her come up with a better solution.

If you can't find out from your child and you think there is a serious problem which has been going on for more than a week, go to step 3.

Step 3: Ask the Teacher

Elementary school teachers spend most of the day with children and often notice when a child needs help. Briefly, and in private, describe to the teacher the changes you have noticed in your child:

MOM: Ann has been getting stomachaches on school days for the past couple of weeks, and she says nothing is the matter. Do you know of anything that might be bothering her?

TEACHER: The group of girls I have this year has been a tough one. They're all so sassy to each other. They're like no other group I've had before. Ann seems to have had a falling out with Amy.

The teacher may not notice what's going on, but may give Ann's mom important information about classmates. That night, about twenty minutes before Ann's bedtime, Mom asks Ann:

MOM: How's Amy doing?
ANN: I don't know.
MOM: Have you talked to her lately?
ANN: No. I don't like her anymore.
MOM: How come?
ANN: She's not very nice.
MOM: What does she do that's not nice?

ANN: She is hanging around with Kim and doesn't want to sit with me at lunch anymore.

Mom then proceeds to help Ann figure out why the girls are avoiding her and what to do about it.

The Next Step

You have learned how to listen to your child so she will tell you problems. You see how your patience has made it easier for your child to talk to you. What do you do about that problem you now know about? Chapters Eighteen to Twenty-Four describe how to help your child with the most common social problems.

18

Having Friends Stolen

———●———

The Problem

- My child believes that one of his best friends has been stolen away by another child who has persuaded him to forsake him. What should I do?

- One of my daughter's friends seems to be trying to get her other friends to avoid her. What should I do?

Background: The Myth of Stealing Friends

Friends are not objects that can be possessed or stolen. A stolen friend is usually the result of poor judgment by both the friend and your child. I'll give you an example of this by showing how Megan's friend Libby was "stolen" by Heather and how Megan could deal with the situation.

Megan, Libby, and Heather, all age eight, are playing together at Libby's house. Megan and Libby are best friends with each other, and Heather is a newcomer. Heather suggests playing hide and seek, with Megan being It. Heather takes Libby aside and says, "Let's hide where Megan can't find us. Let's go to my house [down the street] where she really won't find us." Megan finishes counting and can't find the other girls until they come back from Heather's house ten minutes later.

This is a prime example of why a gracious host is loyal to her guest. (Don't have three on a play date, and don't allow the guest to be left alone; see Chapters Twelve and Thirteen.)

Variations on Heather's behavior are the girl who says, "If you don't do what I want, then I won't be your friend," or "If you hang around with Libby, then I won't be your friend"—what researchers refer to as relational aggression. It has an upsurge in about fourth grade, mainly among girls. Studies show that if it persists beyond this age, it can indicate more serious social problems.[1]

Solving the Problem: Dealing with a Stolen Friend

There are three choices Megan has to handle this, but only one way can turn out well.

Choice A
If Megan overreacts:

MEGAN: [To Libby's mom, crying] Libby left and didn't come back for a long time. I want to go home. Call my mom, please.
LIBBY'S MOM: I'm sure it was a misunderstanding.
MEGAN: I want to go home.

Megan's mom comes to get her while she is still crying and takes her home. Megan is miserable for the next few weeks, having given up on her best friend.

Choice B
If Megan confronts the newcomer, Heather:

MEGAN: Where were you? I looked all over!
HEATHER: We went to my house because I didn't want to play stupid hide and seek.
MEGAN: I don't think that was nice to do.

HEATHER: Well I don't think you're nice. I'm never playing with you again.

There is no friendship between Megan and Heather. Heather feels she has nothing to lose by being unkind to Megan and she might get to play more with Libby alone. Meanwhile, Megan is letting Libby off the hook. The real issue is Libby's loyalty, not Heather's antics.

CHOICE C
If Megan confronts her best friend, Libby:

MEGAN: Where were you? I looked all over!
LIBBY: I went to Heather's house. I thought it was a joke.
MEGAN: I was upset. I thought you left me alone so you could be with Heather.
LIBBY: No, I didn't. I came back.
MEGAN: I don't think that was nice to do.
LIBBY: I'm sorry. I won't do it again. Can we be friends again?
MEGAN: Yes.

Younger children (until about ten or eleven years of age) have a lot to learn about being friends. Sometimes they learn by talks like this last one. Good friends become stronger and more socially competent after they successfully settle disagreements.[2] Good friends

- Quickly settle disagreements.
- Don't leave before a disagreement is settled.
- Once the disagreement is over, let bygones be bygones.

Megan needs to confront Libby (choice C). Here are the steps that Megan's mom follows to get this to happen, starting when she comes to pick her up at Libby's.

Step 1: Get Your Child's Account of What Happened

Use the listening skills (body language, eye contact, voice tone, and opening line) outlined in step 1 of Chapter Seventeen to find out what happened:

> MEGAN'S MOM: Why are you upset?
>
> MEGAN: Libby ran off to Heather's house without telling me and left me alone.
>
> MEGAN'S MOM: That wasn't a nice thing to do. What did you do about it?
>
> MEGAN: I don't want to talk to her. I just want to go home.

Step 2: Have Your Child Confront Her Friend

Megan's mom gets Megan to confront her friend before they go home even if Megan decides she doesn't want to be friends anymore:

> MEGAN'S MOM: You need to tell Libby how you feel about what she did.
>
> MEGAN: But I don't want to be her friend anymore.
>
> MEGAN'S MOM: It doesn't matter. She did something wrong, and you have to tell her. You can decide if you want to be friends after you tell her.
>
> MEGAN: But I don't want to be her friend. She's mean.
>
> MEGAN'S MOM: It doesn't matter. You still have to tell her.

Megan's mom lets Megan and Libby have this conversation by themselves. If Libby apologizes (as usually happens in a case like this), she goes on to step 3. If not, Megan leaves knowing she did her best. Mom praises Megan for trying regardless of how it turned out.

Heather is a different story. If she is not a good friend to Megan or has done this sort of thing several times in the past, then Mom and Megan are cautious about making and accepting play date invitations. If they are good friends and this is the first incident, then she should also be confronted by Megan.

Step 3: On First Offense, Let Bygones Be Bygones

Good friends always deserve a second chance if they rarely make social mistakes with your child:

> MEGAN'S MOM: [In private] What happened when you told her?
> MEGAN: She apologized and said she won't do it anymore.
> MEGAN'S MOM: What do you think about what she said?
> MEGAN: I don't know.
> MEGAN'S MOM: Do you want to give her another chance?
> MEGAN: Okay.
> MEGAN'S MOM: It's nice of you to do that.

Megan's mom's support for the second chance is helpful. If Megan says no, Megan's mom waits to see if Megan will change her mind. If Libby's mom calls about a play date with Megan, she asks Megan before setting it up. However, if Libby makes a habit of forsaking Megan, it's time for Megan to stop trusting Libby.

The Next Step

Helping your child learn to settle disputes by talking them out is a great accomplishment. This is a skill many adults could benefit from learning. But talking things out is not always the best thing to do, as when friends drift apart. The next chapter will show you how to help your child handle this situation.

19

Losing a Close Friend

————————•————————

The Problem

• How can I help my child deal with a friendship that is cooling down?

Background: Losing a Friend

Boys usually have about four or five close friends, and some girls form tighter friendship groups. Girls' friendships are generally more stable than those of boys. Once girls become close friends, they tend to stay friends for several years.

Boys' friendships are generally less intense than girls'. They choose one or two best friends from their favored four or five close friends, and these best friends can change from time to time. Usually a former best friend will stay in the favored four or five. Sometimes one of the favored four or five will drop out of favor for a short period of time. This is a normal pattern to accept in boys.

Sometimes friendships cool down dramatically. There are two common causes for a close friendship to cool down.

The first cause is that they are no longer interested in the same things. Sara and Erin have been friends since the first grade. They are always happy to see each other and have much to tell each other. In fifth grade, Sara becomes very involved in riding, competing, and training horses. This begins to take up a lot of her time, and she begins to hang around other girls she meets at the stable. Sara and Erin's friendship cools off.

Even best friends can drift out of your child's life. Sara and Erin are drifting out of each other's lives right now. The loss of a best friend is a great loss at any age.

The second cause is that they no longer like each other, and one of them gets dumped as a friend, as happened with Josh and George. Josh and George have been best friends since first grade, and their parents are also good friends with each other. In sixth grade, both start attending a small private school. George begins hanging around with a new circle of friends at this school and decides that he no longer wants to be Josh's friend. Josh is crushed. His parents are quite concerned and encourage their son to keep trying to be friends with George. They feel it is important for Josh to be accepted at his new school, especially by George. But the harder Josh tries to be George's friend, the more harshly George treats him and the more the other kids at school tease him. As Josh persists, George becomes more annoyed, and Josh's feelings get hurt even more.

There are early warning signs that best friendships are cooling off. Josh's friendship with George went through three stages in this process:

1. Early stage
    - Josh does most of the inviting for play dates.
    - George frequently declines Josh's invitations.
    - George takes a day or two to accept (accepting only if George is desperate for a play date and has no better offer).
    - George and his mom no longer seem as happy to accept the invitation.

2. Late stage
    * George refuses all of Josh's invitations for play dates.
    * George never invites Josh for a play date.
    * George no longer seeks out Josh at school, but will tolerate him joining in.
3. Point of no return
    * George tells Josh he doesn't want him to hang around.
    * George and others begin to tease Josh for annoying them.

Unfortunately, Josh's persistence forced things to get worse. He finally reached the point of no return and started to look foolish to the other boys by trying to keep George as a friend.

Solving the Problem: Help Your Child Deal with Being Dumped

The best strategy to handle friendships that cool down is to accept the loss and move on.

Step 1: Try to Catch Things at the Early Stage

If you find that a friend shows signs of being in the early stage of cooling off to your child, slow down the invitations to this child:

MOM: It's not a good idea to do all the inviting. Let's wait for George to invite you over next. Who else would you like to invite over to play with tomorrow?

Step 2: Schedule Play Dates with Other Children

Focusing on inviting other children helps turn your child's attention toward these others at school. It also takes the pressure off the friendship that is cooling down so that your child won't try too hard to be friends. He will have a couple of other children to fall back on for play dates and hang around with at school should his relationship reach the late stage of cooling down.

Hold firm to steps 1 and 2 despite your child's desire to see the other child. If you catch this early enough, your child may not lose the friend. Josh's dad talks to Josh about who he sees in school and might ask for a play date. If Josh's dad helps Josh take action before the point of no return, George may want to be Josh's friend again after a while. If it looks as if your child's relationship is headed toward the point of no return, move on to step 3.

Step 3: Help Your Child Grieve for the Lost Friend

Josh's dad gives him his sympathy and lets him grieve:

> JOSH: George told me he doesn't want to be friends anymore.
> JOSH'S DAD: I'm sorry to hear that. Why do you suppose that is?
> JOSH: He's hanging around with others at school I don't like.
> JOSH'S DAD: That's too bad. I lost a best friend once, and it was hard for me.
> JOSH: What can I do?
> JOSH'S DAD: Nothing. You don't have to be friends with George. George found other boys to be friends with, and you will too.

The pressure is off. Josh mopes for a while, and with his parents' encouragement, he begins finding new friends.

The Next Step

It's hard to lose a best friend, but it happens to all of us at one time or another, and there is no easy way to get over it. You have helped your child adjust to the loss. If your child is skilled at making new friends, he will take it from there. If not, follow the steps in Chapter Seven to help him make new friends.

20

Divorce and Moving Away

———●———

The Problem

- We are getting divorced and sharing custody, so part of the time, my child will be away from his friends. What should we do?

- How can I prepare my child for moving away from her friends?

- How can I help my child adjust after moving to a new area?

Background: Cut Adrift After a Move

The loss of friends after a move is especially painful for girls because they make new friends more slowly than boys do.

Ten-year-old Mia is a bright girl who likes to read. She is very close friends with three other girls with similar interests. Her parents are forced to move because of a job change. Mia, naturally quiet, retreats into reading more books instead of making friends with her new classmates. Her parents worry that she is reading too much and that she doesn't have any other girls over.

The other girls in her new class are nice to her, but they are busy with their own friends. Mia does well in school. After a few months, other girls are calling her for homework assignments, and she begins to make new friends.

Everyone in Mia's family feels cut adrift from their friends after the move. But Mia has made friends before and has the social skills to be accepted in her new school: she knows how to make friends and how to behave with close friends.

Children in families who move repeatedly are especially vulnerable after each move. They learn that close friends are only temporary, which hurts their adjustment, especially when they finally settle down in one place.

Twelve-year-old Nancy's family never stays in one place for more than two or three years: since she has been in kindergarten, her family has moved three times. She is a pleasant girl, somewhat quiet. Many children in the school she is in now have had best friends for at least a couple of years. Each time she moves, Nancy mourns the loss of good friends from the previous town, and it's harder for her to get to know new girls. Eventually she meets other girls in school, but best friends are harder to make each time. On this last move, she draws closer to her mother and doesn't make any best friends with other girls.

Divorce is an even more stressful experience for everyone, especially for the parents who are now single and their children. Many divorces not only break apart families, they also tear apart social supports and friendships. Studies show that maintaining best friends may alleviate some of the stress of divorce for children.[1]

Bradley is an eleven-year-old boy whose parents have been divorced for six months. The custody arrangement dictates that Bradley spend two consecutive weeks every month with his father and two weeks with his mother. Bradley has no close friends. One reason is that his father and mother live twenty miles apart, and when he's at his father's house, he can't get together with his friends from school, who live closer to his mother. Bradley's mother is so busy with her job and managing a single-parent household that she does not have time to socialize with other parents and try to arrange play dates. Bradley's father wants to "make the most" of the time he has with his son, so he tries to fill the void of the friends Bradley doesn't see by trying to take their place.

Solving the Problem: Helping Your Child Adjust to the Changes

Many children seek comfort in daily routines. Moving away and divorce disrupt not only daily routines but also support systems and the availability of parents to help their children adjust.

Help Your Child Maintain the Support of Friends After a Divorce

Bradley is isolated at a time he most needs the support of close friends: just after his parents have split up. There are no easy solutions for him. The joint custody arrangement itself was destructive to Bradley's existing friendships, since it didn't permit him to maintain friendships. Nevertheless, there are steps that either or both parents can take that will be helpful to the entire family.

Mom might temporarily put some things on the back burner and help Bradley arrange play dates. Once these get going, she may find it easier to function with a happier eleven year old in the house. When play dates are reciprocated, she will get back this time investment when Bradley is invited to another boy's house. Mom could start by supervising Bradley's calls to friends at her house in the manner described in Chapter Ten. She could also encourage Bradley to use the telephone, IM, and texting when he's at his dad's house to keep in touch with friends from school.

More typical custody arrangements are for Mom to have primary custody and Dad to have the children every other weekend. This is a less disruptive situation where friendships are concerned, but parents still need to take steps to help their child.

Chris is an eight-year-old boy whose parents split up two years earlier. They are still involved in occasional and bitter battles with each other about various issues. However, both parents are alert to the value of play dates and are attentive to Chris when he wants one of his friends to come over to their house. Although Dad lives about fifteen miles from Mom and Chris's friends, he makes great effort to arrange sleepovers well in advance of when Chris comes over to his house. He sometimes picks up another boy when he picks up Chris and offers to drive the boy home after the sleepover.

Help Your Child Adjust to Moving Away from Friends

When I was in my teens, I fell in with a good group of kids: Mark Siedler, who wanted to be a veterinarian; Joe Pruitt, who was a smart kid with a great sense of humor; and Johnny Rodd, who was not too concerned about being cool to have heart-to-heart talks with me. I left to go to college and fell out of touch with them. I still miss them today. It's comforting to know we have friends, even if we don't see them often.

There are three stages that families typically go through with friends when they move:

1. Separation from old friends
2. Mourning the loss of old friends
3. Making new friends

The following steps allow enough time to leave and mourn old friends and then describe how to act quickly to get your child to make new friends.

Step 1: Tell Friends One or Two Months Before You Are Moving

Telling friends one or two months before you move gives everyone time to adjust. Telling your child's friends too soon may start the separation process too early, and parents may put your child last on the list when making play dates. Here is a tactful way to announce you are moving:

LAURA'S MOM: [At the end of a play date with Muriel, to both Muriel and her mom] I'm sorry to tell you that we're moving at the end of the month. Muriel and Laura have been such good friends. I'm sure they're going to miss each other.

MURIEL'S MOM: When are you leaving?

LAURA'S MOM: On May 1. Is it okay if the girls have two more play dates before then, so that they can say good-bye?

MURIEL'S MOM: That's fine. When can we get them together?

The moms then set up both play dates. Children who are good friends will want to keep on playing until the last day. In this way, they give each other the message that they care for each other and the friendship has been worthwhile.

Step 2: Say Good-Bye on a Last Play Date

Ceremonies—weddings, graduations, and saying good-bye before moving away—mark changes in our lives. Sharing our uncertainties as well as our anticipations helps comfort us. Children let go more easily when they exchange mementos to remember each other. The best mementos are inexpensive but have personal meaning. For example, if girls frequently played jump rope together, then a jump rope just like your daughter's would be ideal to give to her best friend.

Step 3: Talk to Your Child About the New Neighborhood

When a former chairperson of my department stepped down, his parting words were, "Change is both a time of loss and a time of opportunity." This is a healthy way to have your child think of the move.

Follow the steps in Chapter Seventeen to listen to your child's worries about moving. Common worries are:

- Will I meet anyone I like?
- Will the other kids like me?

- Will I like my new school?
- Will my new room be as comfortable a place as my
  room is now?

Talk to your child about the new school and neighborhood, and prepare her for the new experiences. Help your child see the move as an opportunity to meet new friends:

MOM: You're going to have your own bedroom in the new house.

SUE: Where's Brooke [her sister] going to sleep?

MOM: She'll be in the room next to you.

SUE: Will there be a place for all my stuffed animals?

MOM: I'll help you make one. Where would you like them?

SUE: How about in a hammock over my bed so they can see me sleeping?

MOM: Okay. Also I noticed that a girl your age lives at the end of the block.

SUE: Does she like to roller-blade?

MOM: I don't know. Maybe you can ask her.

Step 4: Have Your Child Continue to Value Old Friendships

Losing close friends is hard, and many children go into a period of mourning over this loss. Help your child continue to value the friendship, even when it is impossible to continue the friendship.

Chelsea is nine years old and has been friends with Kimberly since kindergarten. Her family moved when she was about to enter fourth grade. She frequently sobs at night during the first three months in her new house, thinking about how much she misses Kimberly.

She feels better when she writes to Kimberly, even though Kimberly never answers her letters. Two years later, although only once hearing from Kimberly, she still regards Kimberly as her best friend.

It is important for Chelsea, as for many other girls I have interviewed, to think of her treasured best friend as permanent. Kimberly is an anchor point in Chelsea's changing world. She may not see Kimberly again or hear from her, but writing makes her feel much better. Sometimes best friends who are separated keep in contact, and sometimes they never write back. Chelsea's mom encourages writing letters, especially soon after the move:

MOM: Why don't you write a letter to Kimberly and tell her how much you miss her?

CHELSEA: I've written Kimberly a letter already, and she hasn't answered me.

MOM: Sometimes just writing helps you feel better. We can decide if you should mail the letter after you write it.

Older girls can stay in contact using IM (see Chapter Eleven), but for younger girls, writing a letter helps them deal with the loss.

Step 5: Use Vacations and Community Resources to Meet New Friends

Although it is typical for children to mourn the loss of their close friends, it is healthy for them to start to meet new friends as soon as possible. Don't wait for them to get over this loss before you try to get them to meet new friends.

Kayla, age eight, has moved to a new neighborhood in which her school is five minutes from her home. Her mother, Tanicka, is on the lookout all summer for activities that children and parents from the new school attend. Tanicka enrolls Kayla in a camp that draws children from her neighborhood. Kayla discovers that Melissa, an eight-year-old playmate at camp, goes to the same school that Kayla will attend. Kayla likes Melissa, and they soon have a play date. Both girls have fun together, and several rewarding play dates follow.

The first week of school, Kayla sees Melissa on the playground during recess and immediately walks over. Kayla and Melissa are thrilled to see each other again.

Starting a new school is stressful for children, especially if they don't know anyone in the new class. Summer is the best time of year for families to move because children have a lot of time to play, and parents are especially willing to make play dates during the week to keep them busy. Tanicka effectively uses community resources over the summer to help Kayla meet others in her new school, and Kayla does the rest.

A good time to make new friends is at the beginning of the school year. Assignment to new classrooms disrupts the friendships children have had the previous year, and many children look around for new friends at this time. Follow the steps in Chapters Four and Five to find and join activities in your new neighborhood.

The Next Step

You have helped your child start over again with friendships after a move or adjust to friendship changes brought about by divorce. Finding new friends will turn this difficult time into an opportunity for your child to master one of life's challenging situations. If your child has had trouble meeting new friends, follow the steps in Chapter Seven. Start looking for children to invite over for play dates, and follow the steps in Chapters Ten and Twelve.

PART FOUR

Dealing with Teasing, Bullying, and Meanness

———•———

Although all three of these problems can be described as victimization, research shows that the causes and the effective responses are very different. Thus, they are addressed in separate chapters.

21

Taking the Fun Out of Teasing

———————●———————

The Problem

• My child is being teased. How can I get this to stop?

Background: Characteristics of Teasing

Teasing is defined as critical remarks directed at another child. It does not include intimidation or threats, the topic of Chapter Twenty-Four, or rumors, which are spread when a child is not present. Rumors are addressed in Chapter Twenty-Two. Studies suggest that teasing is the most common form of victimization in elementary school, where younger children tease primarily by name-calling while older children tease by disparaging the victim or the victim's family.[1]

Teasing can attack the dignity of family members (especially moms, because it hurts more). Anything that will get someone upset, or get laughs at another's expense, will do as a tease. Teasing may be humorous, but the humor is a sarcastic comment made at the expense of the victim, and frequently it is done in front of onlookers. Many victims of teasing also tease others at times.[2]

The dominant motivation reported by teasers is their pleasure at the discomfort of the victim.[3] Children who are effective at stopping teasing employ humor in response to being teased.[4] This response is rated by onlookers as most effective, and the children who use it are rated as friendly and popular.[5]

First-grader Lara, for example, makes her classmate Kim's life miserable. At first Kim joins in playing tag with other children, but Lara is quick to point out that Kim is a slowpoke and calls her dumb. None of the other girls wants to risk being teased along with Kim, so none of them says anything. After a while, Kim asks to stay in at recess, ostensibly to help the teacher, because she is afraid of being teased.

Kim's mother is upset when Kim tells her about the teasing. She knows that if she tries to do anything about it herself, Kim will look worse to the other girls. It would also give Lara something more to tease Kim about and make Kim feel even more awkward.

Why do kids tease? Do they pick on the child who is different just because she is different? This is not the real reason. Two examples will demonstrate this. Both involve overweight second-grade boys, Donald and Timothy:

> *Overweight but not teased:* Donald is clumsy in sports, can't throw a ball well, and runs in an uncoordinated way. He is very polite, well groomed, and considerate of others. He is an average student, enjoys riding his bicycle and skating, and he plays goalie on his soccer team. Several boys always want to make play dates with Donald.

> *Overweight but frequently teased:* Timothy is a pudgy eight year old. Two of his classmates enjoy calling him "Fatty" because when they do, he gets tearful, chases after them, tells them they are not being nice, or threatens to tell the teacher. This makes them laugh. Sometimes he says nothing but hits the teaser, which gets him in trouble with the teacher and yard monitor. Timothy's responses to being teased have made the teasing more fun for the teasing children, since now the children provoke him to hit them in order to get him into trouble.

If being overweight were a reason to be teased, both boys would be teased. No one teases Donald because what he lacks in physical graces he makes up for in social graces, including how to respond to being teased. Children who are constantly being teased don't know how to respond. Before presenting responses to teasing, you should be able to make the distinction between teasing and tactless feedback.

Teasing Versus Tactless Feedback

Ten-year-old Mark wants to be included in all basketball games regardless of the skill level of the other children relative to his. While he was playing with some boys who were much better at basketball than he was, he allowed the ball to be stolen from him while dribbling and missed three shots to the basket, which boys on the opposing team recovered. This distressed the other members of his team. Finally, one boy from his team said to him, "Mark, you stink!"

This was not teasing, where the primary intent was to get Mark upset for the entertainment of the teaser. It was just a tactless way to tell Mark that he had considerably less skill at basketball than the others he chose to play with. A healthy response here was for Mark to play with other boys closer to his skill level in the future so that everyone would have a better time. Dealing with it as teasing would not solve the problem.

Ineffective Responses to Teasing

Children tease because it's fun for them to see someone become upset. Timothy's two classmates get him upset by calling him "Fatty," and he continues to be teased because his responses are babyish and ineffective. Although only a small minority of kids will tease Timothy, some of the other children laugh at his graceless response to being teased. The two children continue teasing Timothy because they enjoy his reaction and they like making the other children laugh at his expense.

Telling the teacher may work in first grade, but by second grade, children view this as babyish and teasing continues ("tattletale"). Walking away from the teaser sometimes works. But what if Timothy or Kim is playing with others? Do they stop playing when they are teased? The key for Timothy and Kim is not to cry, get angry, or shrink from playmates but to learn effective comebacks.

Solving the Problem: Teach Your Child to Make Fun of the Teasing

My experience shows that the most effective technique you can teach your child is to make fun of the teasing: your child makes fun of the teaser's inability to tease well. This is different from teasing back: your child does not sink to the level of the teaser but shows through humor that the teasing does not upset him (even if it does). Children who learn this tell me they have success the first time they use it. They get sympathy from onlookers and take away the fun of teasing.

Mothers are better than fathers at getting their child to practice responses to teasing. If the teasing is about Mom (for instance, "Your mom's fat") and Mom doesn't seem to care about the content ("So what?"), then it takes a lot of the hurt out of the teasing. Your child no longer feels he has to defend the family honor, so he has less reason to be upset when he's teased. Here's how to teach your child what to do.

Step 1: Get as Much Information as You Can About the Teasing

Use the listening skills you learned in Chapter Seventeen to talk about the teasing in a calm, matter-of-fact way. This will help neutralize your child's hurt feelings. Find out who is doing the teasing and as much information about what they are saying as your child will comfortably say. Don't get angry or laugh at the teasing, and don't give advice at this point. Only gather information. Making suggestions too early will end the conversation before you get the information you need.

The best way to neutralize the hurt of teasing is to remain neutral yourself. Don't focus on your child's feelings about being teased. This helps the teaser, since he is succeeding in making your child feel bad and think about how bad he is feeling. Focusing on his feelings will also make it harder for your child to use effective comebacks to teasing. Be patient and let your child tell about it as slowly as he wants:

Mom: How did things go in school today?

Timothy: [Visibly upset] Okay.

Mom: Did something happen today that you would like to tell me about?

Timothy: No.

Mom: Okay.

Timothy: [After ten minutes of silence] The other kids were teasing me again today.

Mom: [In a serious tone] Oh, I see. It happened today?

Timothy: Yes.

Mom: Who teased you today?

Timothy: A whole bunch of kids.

Mom: What did they say?

Timothy: Sam called our family the "fat butts," and the other kids laughed.

Mom: [Serious but neutral tone of voice] Was Sam the only one calling us the fat butts, or was someone else doing it also?

Mom watches Timothy's reaction when she says "fat butts." If Timothy doesn't react, Mom continues to use "fat butts." If Timothy becomes upset, Mom refers to it as "the teasing" after this point:

Timothy: Just Sam, but the rest of the kids laughed.

Mom: Does anyone else tease you besides Sam?

Timothy: No, just Sam, but the other kids laugh.

Timothy had said all the kids tease him, but he now realizes it is only Sam:

Mom: Is this the only thing Sam says to you when he teases you?

Timothy: No. He says I come from the fat family.

Mom: You know, I don't care if Sam calls me fat, so you don't have to worry about me.

Mom makes this last statement (regardless of how accurate it is) after she gathers the facts. It helps Timothy stay calm the next time he is teased. However, this will not be enough to take care of teasing. Sam won't give up unless Timothy makes fun of the teasing.

Step 2: Rehearse Making Fun of the Teasing with Your Child

Teach your child what to say in these situations to take the fun out of teasing with a simple, humorous comeback but without teasing back. Your child will answer every tease with a different reply. When he focuses on the comeback, he will no longer sound hurt and will thus take the fun out of being teased. Read aloud the following list of replies to see if your child likes any of them:

(half-heartedly) "Boo-hoo" (pretending to rub one eye with closed fist).

"So what?"

"Can't you think of anything else to say?"

"I heard that one in kindergarten."

"That's so old it's got dust on it."

"That's so old it's from the stone age."

"I fell off my dinosaur when I first heard that."

"Tell me when you get to the funny part."

"And your point is…"

"Talk to the hand 'cause the face ain't listening."

This is not a complete list. You and your child can probably think of more.

You can now practice how your child will respond to future teasing:

1. Have your child pick ways to make fun of the teasing from the list above or similar statements.

2. Practice several replies to teases, remembering that a mildly disdainful tone of voice is important. Practice each several times.

3. Laugh with your child after each reply he tries.

Making fun of the teasing shows the teaser that your child

- Is not going to cry or get angry.

- Thinks teasing back is beneath him.

- Has an answer for any teasing.

- Is actually having fun delivering the comebacks instead of focusing on the hurt the teaser is trying to inflict.

With a younger child (below third grade), you have to tell him exactly what to say—and keep it simple (only a couple of words). With an older child, try getting him to use replies from the above list of examples or have him come up with his own. Here's how it's done:

Mom: [Reads the above list to Timothy] Want to try any of these? What might you say the next time Sam calls us the fat butts? Remember, don't sink to his level and tease him back. You have to show him teasing is not going to get you angry anymore.

Timothy: [Reads from list without any intonation] "I've heard that one before."

MOM: [Laughing] Yeah, that's a good one [repeats in a confident, mildly disparaging tone of voice]: "I've heard that one before." So what do you say when Sam calls you fatty again?

TIMOTHY: [This time with a little more confidence] "I heard that one before."

MOM: [Laughs] Yeah, that's a good one. Let's try some more. What other one do you like?

TIMOTHY: "That's so old I fell off my dinosaur when I heard it."

MOM: [Laughs] That's great. So what do you say after Sam says you're one of the fat butts?

I find that one session is all the practice most children need.

Step 3: Ask If Your Child Used the Technique and Whether It Worked

I always like to find out how my advice turned out. The next day, Mom has this conversation with Timothy:

MOM: Did you get a chance to try making fun of Sam's teasing?

TIMOTHY: Yeah, he teased me and I said, "So what?" He didn't say anything. He just walked away.

MOM: That's great!

The first time Timothy makes fun of his teasing, Sam will not know what to say next. He will either stop teasing, or when he tries again, he will stop after Timothy comes up with one or two different replies. That's why it is better to rehearse several replies, so that your child will not run out of them before the teaser runs out of teases.

Sometimes children will say the technique didn't work. The two most common errors they make is that they didn't have more than one good comeback and they stumbled over an unrehearsed comeback that ruined the punchline. Both of these errors require you to rehearse more comebacks again.

The Next Step

You've helped your child deal with teasing without your getting into the thick of it. The next chapter shows you how to deal with a tougher form of meanness: rumors.

22

Stopping Rumors

———•———

The Problem

- How can I stop a classmate from gossiping or spreading rumors about my child?

Background: How Rumors Get Started

Gossip helps us learn about the misadventures of others in order to avoid the mistakes they make. It's mostly negative because people can learn more from negative instances.[1]

Children start to gossip as young as four or five years old. Younger children say things like, "Crandall smells bad," about a child who has poor hygiene. Older children are more likely to believe gossip than younger children because they are more likely to realize the utility of gossip as a learning tool.[2] Rumors (negative information about someone) begin in the context of gossip. Denial is the best means to dispel the negative effects of rumors. The best denial has strong arguments about why the rumor isn't true and how the source of the rumor is not credible.[3]

Jenny is a fourth grader who was Elissa's friend and classmate. After a play date at Elissa's house, Elissa noticed that one of her turtles was missing. She decided that Jenny was responsible, although she had left the turtles outside her house, where anyone could take them. The next day, she spread the rumor that Jenny had stolen the turtle. Once the rumor started, most children repeated it to others who hadn't heard it. Many children believed the rumor. Some were unsure, but nevertheless told their friends about it. Many girls started to avoid Jenny because of this rumor. Only two of Jenny's close friends did not believe it and stuck by her. Children were talking about this for the next two weeks.

Social psychologists list three conditions that help a rumor to spread:[4]

1. The children are uncertain about the event in question. If they know it didn't happen, they won't spread the rumor. A child with a reputation of being honest is unlikely to have a rumor spread about her stealing.

2. The children don't care about how true the rumor is. The truth of the rumor doesn't matter to children who aren't Jenny's friends.

3. The rumor is about an issue that worries the children: losing a treasured pet.

Solving the Problem: How to Stop a Rumor That Harms Your Child's Reputation

Rumors eventual die down by themselves, unless either the rumor-monger or the victim does something to keep them going. Here are some approaches to try to have the rumor die down faster.

Step 1: Try to Talk to the Parent of the Child Who Started the Rumor

The best way to stop a rumor is to deal with the child who started it. If Jenny's mom has spoken to the parents of Jenny's playmates before or after each play date (see Chapter Twelve), then she will feel comfortable calling Elissa's mom:

JENNY'S MOM: I hear that Elissa lost one of her turtles. Is that true?

ELISSA'S MOM: Yes. It happened the day Jenny was over.

JENNY'S MOM: Have you found it yet?

ELISSA'S MOM: No. I stopped looking for it after about twenty minutes.

JENNY'S MOM: How do you suppose it was lost?

ELISSA'S MOM: I don't know. It was outside. Maybe it wandered off.

JENNY'S MOM: Does Elissa think that Jenny took it?

ELISSA'S MOM: She mentioned that.

JENNY'S MOM: We don't have any turtles here. You know me: I wouldn't tolerate her taking it.

ELISSA'S MOM: That's true.

JENNY'S MOM: What concerns me is that a rumor has spread at school that Jenny took the turtle and they're all in a stew about it.

ELISSA'S MOM: I'll talk to Elissa.

JENNY'S MOM: Thanks. That would be a great help.

Jenny's mom patiently and politely gathers information, and both moms are in agreement. Now Elissa's mom can stop Elissa from feeding the rumor. Go to step 2 only if this doesn't work.

Step 2: Talk to the Supervising Adult

It would indeed be a wonderful world if we could always talk out our problems directly with each other. But sometimes we can't, either because we don't know who started a rumor or the other parent will not listen to reason. Since this rumor is spreading in the classroom, the teacher is the ideal person to intervene. If she is unaware of what is going on, it is up to Jenny's mom to alert her. Here's how she does this:

MOM: Jenny is upset about a rumor being spread about her. Have you heard about it?

TEACHER: No, I haven't, but it wouldn't be the first time this has happened. I have trouble with this every year.

MOM: The girls are talking about Jenny stealing a turtle from her playmate. I didn't notice any turtles at our house and the turtles were left out in front of the girl's house, where they could have walked away on their own. Jenny is very upset about it. Several other girls keep talking about this, and they are avoiding Jenny over it. Do you have any suggestions about what should be done to help this situation?

The important things Jenny's mom does are:

- She avoids naming Elissa. Clearly she isn't going to start a rumor about Elissa.
- She calmly explains how the rumor isn't true.
- She calmly informs the teacher of Jenny's social situation.
- She asks the teacher for help rather than telling the teacher what to do. Many school personnel will feel situations like this are their business if it impairs school work.

Jenny's mom stands a good chance of getting the teacher to help. In response, the teacher gives the class a lecture about spreading rumors: how they hurt kids whether or not they are true, and how false stories can be believed even when the person telling them has no firsthand knowledge of what happened. She prohibits all rumors. The rumors about Jenny stop, and Jenny's relationships with her classmates soon return to normal.

Jenny's teacher used an effective approach. If your child is facing the same problem and the teacher refuses to intervene, you will have to let the rumor die down of its own accord. In other words, say and do nothing more about it. Children forget eventually if nothing happens to remind them.

The Next Step

You have used the most effective way to deal with rumors. Rumors like the one Elissa started can make children and parents feel help-less. Learning how to deal with rumormongers is an important life skill. The next chapter shows you how to help your child deal with being physically hurt by other children.

23

Staying Away from Children Who Fight

———•———

The Problem

- How can I help my child avoid being physically hurt by another child?

Background: Children Who Fight and Children Who Bully

First, figure out if the other child is a child who fights or a child who bullies. You might ask, "Aren't they the same? Even if they aren't, what difference does it make?" Fighters and bullies in fact are not the same, and it will help you to know which one is picking on your child so you can take the best action.

No child deserves to picked on by a child who fights or bullies, but fighting and bullying call for different responses. Decide from Table 23.1 which one is giving your child a problem. If the child is bullying, read the next chapter. If the child is a fighter, read on.

Phillip, age seven, likes to play with others at recess. John, a much taller, heavier, and stronger boy, is his harasser. John gets into frequent physical fights with others, and lately he has been hitting Phillip a lot.

Table 23.1   Characteristics of Children Who Pick on Others

Characteristics of Children Who Fight	Characteristics of Children Who Bully
Are disliked by most other children	Have a circle of friends who bully with them
Will fight with anyone	Pick on children who are alone, weaker than they are, and won't complain
Don't intentionally pick on any particular child	Pick on the same child repeatedly
Will fight at any time	Pick on a child when adults aren't watching
Physically hurts others in order to settle disputes	Are cruel to other children in order to control them
Fight because they misunderstand social cues	Pick on others because they enjoy seeing their reaction

Sources: For fighting: Patterson, G. R., DeBaryshe, B. D., & Ramsey, E. (1989). A developmental perspective on antisocial behavior. *American Psychologist, 44,* 329–335. For bullying: Olweus, D. (1993). Bullies on the playground: The role of victimization. In C. H. Hart (Ed.), *Children on playgrounds* (pp. 45–128). Albany: State University of New York Press.

John barges into a game Phillip is playing and takes the ball. Phillip's response is to tearfully approach John and tell him to stop, while the other children say nothing. In response, John laughs and hits Phillip.

As a father, it gets my adrenaline going when I hear that someone has picked on my son. I understand how other dads could feel the same way. Even if Phillip's parents encourage Phillip to fight back or send him to karate lessons, it won't stop children like John from hurting children like Phillip. The first time Phillip tries to fight back, he will lose. Phillip will not only feel picked on by John, but will also feel inferior because he can't succeed in an area his parents feel is important.

It's a mistake to try to teach Phillip to fight. Phillip's parents would be giving him the wrong message: that fighting is okay and what John is doing is acceptable. Phillip is not a fighter. He happens to be considerate of others' feelings and doesn't settle arguments with physical force. You've brought him up that way; keep him that way, and he'll go far in life (bless his heart).

Solving the Problem: Avoiding the Fighter

Phillip's dad teaches Phillip to stop calling attention to himself when he tells John to stop. He should not take John on by himself. Here's how to teach your child to avoid the fighter.

Step 1: Get All the Details from Your Child

Once again, the steps in Chapter Seventeen come in handy to get the details of the fight from your child:

PHILLIP: John is picking on me at recess.
DAD: What does he do?
PHILLIP: He takes the ball away when I'm playing with my friends, and he chases me and hits me.
DAD: Does John get into fights with other kids too?
PHILLIP: Yes. No one likes him.

Phillip's answers establish that John is a child who fights (left column of the table), not a child who bullies. Dad gets the whole incident from Phillip:

DAD: What do you do when he takes the ball away?
PHILLIP: I walk over to him and tell him to give it back.
DAD: Does he give it back?
PHILLIP: No. He hits me instead.
DAD: You are right—he should give it back. But telling him doesn't seem to work. Do you want to try something different to see if it will help?

Dad doesn't criticize Phillip for what he did. Also, before giving a suggestion, he makes certain Phillip is ready to hear it. If Phillip says, "No!" to this question, Dad makes no suggestion. He says only, "What John is doing is wrong. Let me know if you want me to help you figure out what to do next time."

Step 2: Teach Your Child How to Avoid the Fighter

Five rules will help Phillip avoid John:

1. Don't talk to John.
2. Hang out with a group of your friends (a group is more difficult for a fighter to approach than a child who is playing alone).
3. Protect yourself by staying out of John's reach.
4. Play close to the yard monitor when you can.
5. Don't tease John or make faces at him.

One of my main mottoes in life is, "If it works, keep doing it, and if it doesn't, try something else." Here's how Dad and Phillip decide what Phillip will try next time John bothers him:

PHILLIP: Okay, what should I do?

DAD: Next time he takes the ball away, do nothing. Don't talk to him, and see if he gets tired of having the ball.

PHILLIP: But it's my ball!

DAD: That's right. But John really has no use for it, since no one wants to play with him. He's only using it to get you to fight with him.

PHILLIP: What if he hits me?

DAD: Well, how about trying to keep out of his reach?

PHILLIP: Okay.

DAD: Give it a try and see what happens. I'll ask you tomorrow if it helped.

Dad doesn't try to convince Phillip that it will work. He leaves it to Phillip to try it himself. This way, if it doesn't work, Phillip can tell his dad about it the next day and get some more help (Dad has one more suggestion up his sleeve).

Step 3: Ask Later to See If It Worked

Now it is up to Dad to ask whether Phillip tried either of these suggestions and whether they helped. He praises Phillip for trying what he suggested even if it didn't work.

PLAN A

If it worked, praise him:

DAD: Did John bother you again today?
PHILLIP: He did. But I didn't get close to him, and he didn't hit me.
DAD: That's great. I'm glad to see you're not getting hurt!
PHILLIP: But John shouldn't do stuff like that.
DAD: You're right. But you did the right thing.

PLAN B

If it didn't work, find something to praise in what your child tried and suggest another approach from step 2:

PHILLIP: He bothered me. I did what you said and didn't say anything. But he chased me anyway.
DAD: Did he hit you?
PHILLIP: No. But I couldn't get back in the game.

DAD: I'm glad you tried not talking to him and he didn't hit you. Do you want to get your friends to play near the yard monitor next time?

PHILLIP: Okay. I'll tell my friends.

Give your child a chance to try it out and ask again about how it worked.

The Next Step

You have fought your initial instincts to get directly involved when your child has been annoyed by a child who fights. You've helped your child learn to do this without violence. Nonviolent responses are the safest to use with potentially violent people.

Your child will be more protected from the fighter if he hangs out with a group of friends. If your child doesn't have friends to hang out with, help him to find new friends using the steps described in Chapters Seven, Ten, and Twelve.

24

Dealing with Children Who Bully

———•———

The Problem

- How can I help my child when she is bullied by another child?

Background: How to Tell If Your Child Is Being Bullied

Children who bully others do so to varying degrees. Children younger than fifth or sixth graders bully in person. Older children begin to use cell phones and the Internet to bully, harass, and intimidate. In mild cases, a bully occasionally ridicules or threatens another child. In extreme cases, a bully systematically and thoroughly humiliates another child. Fortunately, mild cases are more common. Your child will talk to you about being mildly bullied when you use the listening techniques in Chapter Seventeen. If you act quickly, bullying will not become severe.

Severe bullying is different and uglier. The usual way that bullying becomes severe is that the child who is bullied doesn't tell anyone else it's happening for several reasons:

- It's humiliating, and they are too embarrassed to talk about it.
- They feel that no one else will understand or believe them.
- They feel that if anyone tried to help, it would only make the situation worse.
- If it is happening with a cell phone, they are afraid their parents will take away their cell phone.

If you notice certain changes in your child's behavior, you will have to do some detective work to find out about severe bullying. Here are some signs:[1]

1. Your child's school work begins to slide.
2. Your child shows much less interest in schoolwork than usual.
3. Your child does not want to go to school or starts having frequent stomachaches or headaches on school days.
4. If your child walks to school, she changes her usual path to an out-of-the-way route.
5. Your child's books, money, or other belongings are missing without explanation.
6. Your child begins stealing or requesting extra money for lunch.
7. Your child begins to have unexplained injuries or torn clothing.

The first three signs are general signs of distress about something at school, while the last four are specific to being bullied.

Cyberbullying has arisen with the greater use of the Internet by children. One survey found that 16 percent of children between the ages of eleven and nineteen were harassed by text messaging, 7 percent were harassed in Internet chat rooms, and 4 percent were harassed by e-mail.[2]

The most effective response to this form of harassment is to not respond. E-mail programs have filters that block or automatically delete messages from undesirable senders. It is also possible to trace from which e-mail account the offending message was sent. IM programs allow users to create a list of others from which users may wish to block messages.

It is usually better to have school administrators deal with cyberbullying. It has been recommended that "a provision be added to the school's acceptable use policy reserving the right to discipline students for actions conducted away from school if such actions have an adverse effect on a student or if they adversely affect the safety and well-being of the student while in school."[3]

Solving the Problem: Neutralize the Bully

The power equation for bullying is usually on the side of the bully. That's why it is necessary for parents to take charge of this situation and act decisively so that the victim will have confidence that something can be done to improve his or her situation.

Step 1: Get as Much Detail as Possible from Your Child

Use the techniques described in Chapter Seventeen to get details from your child on times when she has been bullied. It will be easier for your child to talk about mild bullying than if she has been more severely bullied. Be careful not to make your child feel any worse; avoid addressing why she didn't tell you of the bullying. The fact that you could and would do something about the bullying that helped will get your child to confide in you more.

Responses to bullying are different for mild bullying than for more serious bullying. We start with a mild case in this example.

Seven-year-old Victor tells his mother that he doesn't want to go to school anymore. When she asks why, he says, "Because I don't want to be near Julian." Upon further questioning, Victor tells his mother that Julian demands his desserts each day. He also demands piggy-back rides and tells him what games to play.

Victor is bullied because he is very compliant. He tells his mother what's going on, and she responds by telling Victor not to listen to Julian:

MOM: Suppose another boy like Julian tells you to give him your dessert and you don't want to. Do you really have to do it?

VICTOR: No.

MOM: Let's think of something you could do. Could you say no?

VICTOR: Yes. But what if he tries to take it?

MOM: Just say no again, and pull the dessert out of his reach. Let's try it. I'll be Julian. "I want that dessert."

VICTOR: "No."

MOM: "But I have to have that dessert!"

VICTOR: What do I do now?

MOM: Say no again only a little louder. Try it.

VICTOR: [In a firmer and louder voice] "No!"

MOM: [Whispering] That's great. [and then in role-playing Julian] "You need to give me that dessert."

VICTOR: "NO!"

MOM: That was great!

David, age eight, is walking home from school by the swamp when he encounters three boys playing. One boy demands that he walk across the swamp to the other side. Without a thought of doing anything else, he walks through the swamp. The water is up to his chest in parts, and he comes home with his pants and shirt muddy.

David makes the same mistake that Victor does: he obeys the bullies. Disobeying does not mean fighting; it means not waiting for the three boys to act. It is important for David not to give the bully control of the situation.

David thinks that running away is more humiliating than what he did. He is wrong. He gives the three boys the notion that they can control him. Here's how David's dad helps him refuse the next time this happens:

DAD: What could you do next time someone tells you to do something like that? Suppose there are three boys and only one of you?

DAVID: I don't know.

DAD: Well, let's see. There are three of them. Can you run somewhere nearby where there's an adult?

DAVID: But they'd call me chicken!

DAD: I think that would be a smart thing to do. There are three of them, and only one of you. I think they are the cowards.

This next example shows a more severe case of bullying. Elise is one of the smartest girls in her fifth-grade class. Her friendship group fluctuates between two and five girls. Their common interests are making fun of overweight people and children not as smart as they are. Elise picks on Rebecca constantly, teasing her about her parents, calling them "the stupid family." She also tells the other girls not to play with Rebecca. They are afraid not to cross Elise for fear they will be targets. She "borrows" money from Rebecca, promising to be a true friend. When Rebecca gives her money, Elise never pays her back. When Rebecca refuses to give money, Elise threatens that her big sister will beat up Rebecca.

Rebecca's mother notices that she is coming home from school very hungry. She also is refusing to do her homework because she says it's too hard. Her grades have started slipping, and she frequently complains of stomachaches before going to school each day. Here's how Rebecca's mom gets to the bottom of this:

REBECCA: I don't feel like going to school today. I feel sick.

MOM: I'm worried about you, Rebecca. You've been having stomachaches in the morning, and you seem pretty hungry when you come home from school. Is something wrong with the school lunches?

REBECCA: The lunches are okay. I'm just not hungry at lunchtime.

Rebecca's mom shows concern and now focuses on one small part of what she has been noticing in order not to overwhelm Rebecca. She continues:

MOM: So you aren't buying lunch?

REBECCA: No.

MOM: What do you do with the money I give you every day?

REBECCA: Elise asks me for my lunch money.

MOM: Do you give it to her?

REBECCA: Sometimes.

MOM: Why do you give it to her?

REBECCA: Because if I don't, Elise says her sister will get me.

MOM: Is she alone when this happens?

REBECCA: No. Two other girls are usually with her.

Step 2: Take Charge and Do the Tattling

This is one of the few times I will tell you to take charge and tattle on the bully. Rebecca does not want to call attention to herself, either because of what other children might think or her fear that Elise's older sister will hurt her. Mom tells the teacher in private what is going on:

MOM: [After school when the teacher is alone] Can I get your advice on something that's been bothering Rebecca for quite some time now?

TEACHER: What is it?

MOM: Rebecca's having trouble coming to school and comes home hungry because a couple of girls are demanding her lunch money. She says that if she doesn't give it to them, they threaten to hurt her.

TEACHER: Who is doing this?

MOM: I have trouble believing this, but Rebecca says it's Elise.

TEACHER: I cannot believe that Elise would do such a thing.

MOM: I have trouble believing it also, but Rebecca usually doesn't lie. Could you do some checking to see if there's anything to this? Rebecca also says that Elise has been telling the other girls not to play with her.

TEACHER: Certainly.

MOM: Shall I check back with you in a couple days to see what you found out?

TEACHER: Okay.

In this conversation, Rebecca's mom is asking for help, not telling the teacher what to do. In addition, she initially doesn't say who it is doing the bullying, so the teacher can more clearly hear what's going on. Elise is one of the smartest girls in the class, and the teacher may have trouble hearing negative things about her.

This is a worst-case scenario where the child who is bullying is a favored student. Mom has to be patient because it's Rebecca's word against Elise's. In Victor's case, a word to the teacher brings immediate action, because Julian's behavior is rather obvious.

Very rarely teachers will not think it is their business to become involved in cases of bullying. This is a serious mistake, because not being involved condones bullying. If your child's teacher feels this way, meet with the school psychologist or principal. Use this meeting to discuss school policy. Because of the legal liability and increased awareness of the problem, many school officials feel they have to listen when a child is being bullied. If this doesn't work, you will have to get an attorney. Usually a letter from an attorney is enough to show that you will press the issue until the bullying stops. Sometimes the issue is one child's word against another and administrators have an obligation to ask for proof. It's helpful to have other witnesses or tangible evidence.

Step 3: Protect the Victim from the Bully

Check frequently with the teacher or school officials to see how they are following up. A couple of telephone calls to them should be enough. Since your child was the victim, you have a voice in how they will protect your child in the future. Make some suggestions—for example:

- Elise writes a letter of apology to Rebecca rather than apologize face-to-face. Because Elise has controlled Rebecca by terrorizing her, she could use intimidating glances and tone of voice even if she is made to apologize in person.
- Elise is penalized if she is caught within twenty feet of Rebecca. This gives the message that what Elise did to Rebecca was wrong and Rebecca was right to tell an adult. Rebecca feared that telling people would make it worse. She needs to be shown that the adults can keep Elise away from her.

Step 4: Have Your Child Hang Out with Friends

Hanging out with a group of friends will discourage bullies. Help your child make arrangements to do this.

The Next Step

Acting decisively toward bullying is the best way you can help your child in this situation. Being bullied by a group of children has negative long-term effects on both the bullies and the victims.

Your child will be better protected from the bully if he hangs out with a group of friends during recess and while going to and from school. If your child doesn't have friends to hang out with, help him to find new friends using the steps described in Chapters Seven, Ten, and Twelve. In the meantime, take him to and from school, or make other arrangements where he won't be alone at these times. Continue to follow up to see that the school is keeping the bully away from your child.

PART FIVE

Helping Your
Child Out
of Trouble

———————•———————

Some children have no friends. Some bully or fight with other children, and some constantly get into trouble with adults. If this describes your child, you're probably feeling upset and helpless. It's time to take action.

25

Working with Adults Who Have Trouble with Your Child

———————●———————

The Problem

- Why do some adults have a problem with my child? What is it about her?
- How can I stop my child from talking back to her teacher, coach, and other adults?
- How can I stop an adult supervisor from picking on my child?

Background: Children Who Challenge Adults

If a teacher is interesting and the material is pitched to their level of understanding, most children sit quietly and listen. But a few children don't and challenge the supervising adult. Some children are liked by classmates despite this behavior. But for others, this behavior damages their reputation.

In order to help you understand why one child is liked and the other disliked, here are two examples of children who interrupt when an adult is teaching. In the examples, both children are working on sand painting in the same classroom.

Nick, age nine, is a child who talks back but has friends. He makes frequent remarks that make fun of what the supervising adult tells him to do. The other children laugh at his comments. For example, he might say to the instructor, "If we make that sand painting, can we go on vacation?" and to another child who is trying to draw the sun in his picture, he might say, "That's a nice pinwheel you made."

He does his own version of sand painting, sprinkling sand all over the paper. Then he starts horsing around with another child, both throwing a little sand on each other while smiling. Nick horses around several times each hour. Each time, the supervising adult tells him to stop. Each time, he listens to the adult by the first or second request.

Nick is a minor pain in the neck to the supervising adult, but he helps to make the activity more enjoyable for the other children. I've known some adults who are very tolerant of children (some teachers are my superheroes in this regard) and some adults who should never be around any child. Some teachers are well suited to teach classrooms of reasonably behaved children but fly apart when they have a child who constantly talks back. Nick doesn't get along with some of his teachers.

Monty, is also nine years old, and is a child who talks back but is friendless. He makes frequent belittling comments about the supervising adult's instructions: "That's stupid," or "That's boring," or "I don't want to do that." When the time comes to work on the craft, he is unsure what to do and frequently demands help while the supervising adult is busy helping another child.

While reaching for some glue, another child accidentally bumps him. His angry response is, "You messed up my work; now I'm going to mess up yours." He then throws sand at the other child and his project. The other child becomes upset.

If your child talks back to adults, you are in a tough position. Through no fault of your own, you find yourself talking to an adult who is upset about your child's behavior. You want his understanding and cooperation not his anger.

When an adult complains to you, you have two objectives: work together with the complaining adult and help your child stop the offensive behavior. In this chapter I address the child who talks back. Chapter Twenty-Six gives some additional help if your child is getting into physical fights with other children.

Solving the Problem: Work Together with the Complaining Adult

In this situation, you reassure the adult that you will help him with the problem. Here's how.

Step 1: Talk to the Complaining Adult

Talking to the complaining adult may begin to defuse the situation, as it did in this situation with nine-year-old Kathy, who is in an after-school swim program. She constantly gets into trouble with the lifeguard for horsing around in the pool. Finally the lifeguard has had enough and tells her he is never going to allow her in the pool again. From now on, she must sit on the sidelines and watch other children enjoying themselves.

Kathy's defiance has frustrated the lifeguard. Kathy's parents have not spoken to him about this, and without anywhere to turn, he finally has taken drastic action.

Kathy's mom or dad calls the lifeguard and defuses this situation by following these guidelines:

1. Be polite. Check if you are talking to the adult at a convenient time for him.
2. Stay calm.
3. Ask for specifics. Ask for the adult's side of the issue, whether or not you think your child was at fault. The adult has important information you haven't heard.
4. Express your concern about the issue and your availability to work together with the adult.

5. Arrange to keep communication open. This is the best
    way you show that you are taking the problem seriously
    and are not leaving the supervising adult alone to work
    on it.

Kathy's dad makes the call:

DAD: Hello, this is Kathy's dad. Is this a convenient time for
you to talk?
LIFEGUARD: Yes. I've been wanting to talk to you about Kathy.
That girl has serious problems!

The lifeguard's complaint is out of proportion to what Kathy
has done, but he is clearly frustrated. Dad stays calm and asks for
specifics:

DAD: What has she been doing?
LIFEGUARD: When the kids get into the pool, she starts horsing
around and mouths off to me when I tell her to stop. I have fifteen
other children to supervise, and I can't be playing policeman just
for her.
DAD: I realize you have the safety of all of the children in mind.
Is there anything I can do to help?
LIFEGUARD: Kathy needs to listen to me the first time I
tell her.
DAD: I agree. I will have a talk with her. Can I get daily reports
from you on whether she listens?
LIFEGUARD: That sounds good.
DAD: Great! I'll ask you each time I pick her up. If she doesn't
listen to you, I will take away a privilege when she gets home. I
think she'll get the message if we both work together.

Dad's suggestion makes the lifeguard less angry at Kathy, and
it gives the lifeguard an alternative to permanently excluding her.

*Step 2: When You Get Home, Get Your Child to Talk About
the Troublesome Incident*

Kathy's dad asks for her view of the incident with the lifeguard.
He does this to help her plan what she will do the next time this
happens. He says nothing supportive of what she did (unless she
describes ways she tried to avoid conflict). He follows these guidelines when talking to Kathy:

- Don't accuse your child of being in the wrong. This
  will get you nowhere and will make it difficult for your
  child to continue the conversation.

- Don't dispute your child's side of the story or say, "Tell
  the truth!" This will take you off track, and you will
  never know the truth. What matters most is that your
  child doesn't repeat the offense.

- Don't say anything disrespectful about the adult. Be a
  model of respect toward this adult, even if the adult is
  wrong. Always give the adult the benefit of the doubt
  unless he or she is physically hurting or verbally
  abusing your child.

- Don't lecture. Your child will tune you out after you
  say the first few words.

Here's how it's done:

DAD: The lifeguard tells me you weren't listening to him today.
KATHY: He accused me of something I didn't do.
DAD: What did he say?
KATHY: He said I was throwing floaties in the pool without
asking first.
DAD: Were you? And what did you say?
KATHY: I said, "I did not! You always blame me for things that
other kids do!"

DAD: Saying that got you kicked out of the pool. What would you do differently next time?

KATHY: But he was wrong!

DAD: If you want to keep swimming in the pool, you'll have to listen to him.

KATHY: But he was wrong!

DAD: He is an adult, and you need to show respect for an adult.

Step 3: Have Your Child Think of Better Ways to Handle the Incident

Your main task is to have your child think of better ways to handle the problem. There are three rules your child should follow in this situation:

1. Explain the situation to the adult only once.
2. If this doesn't work, stop talking, even if you think the adult is wrong.
3. Don't get angry, answer back, give dirty looks, or roll your eyes. An adult won't listen if you're disrespectful.

Kathy's dad teaches her these rules so she won't talk back:

DAD: Next time the lifeguard accuses you, I want you to explain yourself only once, then stop talking and be respectful. Let's pretend I'm the lifeguard and I just thought I saw you throwing floaties in the pool. I say, "Stop that! Out of the pool for five minutes." What are you going to do?

KATHY: But I didn't do it.

DAD: So what do you say to the lifeguard?

KATHY: "I didn't do it, but I'll stay out for five minutes."

DAD: Good! Then what would you do?

KATHY: Stay out for five minutes.

DAD: That's great. I like that you told your side only once and didn't argue. Also, show me how you would look at the lifeguard when you are talking.

KATHY: [Looks with straight face]

DAD: Good. You're not making any faces. Try it out next time it happens. If you listen to him next time, even if you think he was wrong, you won't get into more trouble. Tell me what happens.

Secure a promise from your child to do this next time. If he does, praise him for this. If your child refuses to engage in this conversation, go to the next step anyway.

Step 4: Give an Immediate, Brief Penalty After Each Instance of Talking Back to an Adult

You make your point effectively when you give your child a brief penalty after each instance of talking back to the adult.

• • •

1. The penalty should be brief—no longer than one or two hours. The idea is not to make the penalty fit the crime, but to make the penalty just strong enough so your child will not repeat the behavior. You are looking for a steady decrease in talking back (for example, from once a week to once every two weeks), so that after a few penalties, your child is no longer talking back. Never use any kind of physical response that will cause your child pain as a penalty.

2. Penalty time should not be fun: no games, TV, pleasant conversation, team sport, scout meeting, or anything else. If there is a movie you were planning to go to, it's canceled.

If your child had a play date, make the penalty last until the play date (otherwise, you're also punishing your child's friend). If the play date will start too soon, give the penalty after the play date.

3. State the exact penalty before beginning it: "For talking back today, you have no TV or games until 6:00 P.M."

4. After the penalty is over, do not discuss it further. Wipe the slate clean.

5. Don't ask for an apology from your child. Sometimes children feel that an apology makes it okay to repeat the behavior again. The only way things get better is not to repeat the behavior. Give this penalty every time your child gets in trouble, including the first time. Most children will accept a penalty for behavior they know is not acceptable.

Step 5: Check Back with the Complaining Adult

Keep track of the number of incidents by getting daily or weekly reports from the complaining adult. If the number amounts to several each week, keep track of weekly totals.

PLAN A
If weekly totals decrease, congratulations! Keep it up. You're on the right track!

PLAN B
If weekly totals increase or stay the same for three weeks, seek professional help.[1]

• • •

This is a lot to remember, so I have put this together into the following checklist.

✓ *Checklist for Working with Adults Who Have Trouble with Your Child* ✓

Step 1: Talk to the complaining adult.
- Be polite. Check if you are talking to the adult at a convenient time for him.

- Stay calm.

- Ask for specifics.

- Express your concern about the issue and your availability to work together with him or her.

- Arrange to keep communication open.

Step 2: When you get home, talk to your child about the troublesome incident.
- Don't accuse your child of being in the wrong. This will get you nowhere and make it difficult for your child to continue the conversation.

- Don't dispute your child's side of the story or say to your child, "Tell the truth." This will take you off-track, and you will never know the truth. What matters most is that your child doesn't repeat the offense.

- Don't say anything disrespectful about the adult. Be a model of respect toward this person, even if he or she is wrong. Always give the adult the benefit of the doubt, except if the adult is physically hurting or verbally abusing your child.

- Don't lecture. Your child will tune you out after you say the first few words.

Step 3: Have your child think of better ways to handle the incident.

- There are three rules your child should follow in this situation:

1. Explain the situation to the adult only once.

2. If this doesn't work, stop talking, even if you think the adult is wrong.

3. Don't get angry, answer back, give dirty looks, or roll your eyes. An adult won't listen if you're disrespectful.

Step 4: Give an immediate, brief penalty after each instance of talking back.

1. The penalty should be brief—no longer than one or two hours. Never use any kind of physical response that will cause your child pain as a penalty.

2. Penalty time should not be fun. If your child had a play date, make the penalty last until the play date (otherwise you're also punishing your child's friend). If the play date will start too soon, give the penalty after the play date.

3. State the exact penalty before beginning it.

4. After the penalty is over, do not discuss it further. Wipe the slate clean.

Step 5: Check back with the complaining adult.

Plan A: If weekly totals decrease: Keep it up. You're on the right track!

Plan B: If weekly totals increase or stay the same: If this happens for three weeks, seek professional help.

The Next Step

Talking back to adults is a difficult problem to deal with. As with other trying times of being a parent, your patience and persistence have paid off. If your child is fighting with others, read the next chapter.

26

Stopping Your Child's Fighting

---•---

The Problem

- The teacher says my child fights at school. What should I do to find out what's going on?

- How can I stop my child from getting into physical fights?

Background: Children Who Fight

Six-year-old Jimmy has no friends in school. One time he is waiting to use the classroom computer with Andy, his classmate. Jimmy leans on Andy while he is waiting. Jimmy has done this before to Andy, and Andy has seen other children having trouble with Jimmy. In his frustration, he screams at Jimmy to get away from him. Jimmy steps on Andy's foot hard as he is leaving, and Andy begins to cry. This is the third child Jimmy has hurt this week, and the teacher sends him to the principal.

The principal calls Jimmy's parents and tells them what has been happening. On the way home, Jimmy tells his version of what happened: "Andy was mean to me for no reason, and when I tried to get away from him, I accidentally stepped on his foot."

Jimmy's parents make the mistake of believing Jimmy's version of what happened, despite the fact that he has hurt several other children recently. They do nothing more about it, and the situation continues. Jimmy hurts whoever irritates him but is not aware that he irritates his classmates. He is aware that no one likes him and that the kids tease him and pick on him. His parents are not aware of what Jimmy does to provoke others.

Children outgrow many behaviors, but fighting gets worse with age.[1] Some parents tell me, "I was like this when I was younger, and I turned out okay." But studies show that the child who fights is at higher risk for later serious social problems, such as delinquency and school dropout.[2] Other parents tell me they are painfully aware of their child's fighting but don't think there is anything they can do about it. When parents see fighting as a serious problem and follow the next steps, they can help their child to stop fighting.

Solving the Problem: Help Your Child Find Better Ways to Solve Problems

Most fighting occurs when parents are not watching. Rather, they hear about it from complaining adults and from their child. The basic steps are the same as in Chapter Twenty-Five, but you need more help for handling your child's fighting.

Step 1: Listen to the Complaining Adult

Children who fight don't usually tell their parents and don't admit their part in it. The first time you hear about it is when you are told by an adult who is supervising your child.

Sometimes parents of a child who fights tell me their child doesn't fight at home, and so they have trouble believing it is a real problem. They think

- Maybe the other children are starting the fights and their child is striking back in self-defense.

- Maybe the teacher is picking on their child because the teacher doesn't like their child. Teachers may get angry at a child who fights because they feel helpless to control it and feel an obligation to protect the victims.

- Maybe it's normal for boys to get into fights. But in fact, only 5 to 10 percent of boys get into fights.[3]

Your first and most important step is to listen to the complaining adult. Follow the guidelines in step 1 of Chapter Twenty-Five to deal effectively with the complaining adult. Acknowledge the problem and agree to work with the adult until it is no longer a problem:

TEACHER: Your son hit George Mayberry this morning.

MOM: What happened?

TEACHER: I didn't see it start, but this is the third child John hit this week.

MOM: I'm surprised. He doesn't fight at home. He's going to be grounded tonight for it.

TEACHER: I should think so.

MOM: I want this to stop. Can I get a report from you each day after school? Anytime I find he has hit someone, I will ground him. I want him to get the message that what he is doing is wrong.

Step 2: Get Your Child to Talk About the Troublesome Incident

As in the previous chapter, when you get home, listen to your child's side of the incident. You are doing this for three reasons. You want

- Your child to be clear on why he is being grounded.

- To make it clear that there are no good excuses for fighting.

• Him to think of other things he can do instead of
  fighting.

Don't support any justification he gives unless it was about an attempt to avoid fighting. Here's how you begin:

MOM: Your teacher told me you got into a fight with George at school today.

JOHN: He started it.

MOM: What happened?

JOHN: I was minding my own business. Out of nowhere, George came over and took my ball away. I didn't hurt him. I just got my ball back.

Don't get sidetracked by disputing your child's side of the story. You are getting your child to start thinking about the situation that led to the fight.

Step 3: Have Your Child Think of Better Ways to Handle the Incident

Help your child to think of nonaggressive ways to handle the problem. Here are some examples:

The Provocation	Your Response
Another child is playing with a toy he doesn't know belongs to you.	Tell him that it's yours.
Another child frequently takes away your ball or toy.	Younger children: Tell an adult.
	Older children: Show no reaction (they're just trying to get you upset).

Another child teases you.	Use the "make fun of the teasing" technique" in Chapter Twenty-One.
Another child hits or pushes you.	Stay out of arm's reach, hang around with other kids, or stay near the yard monitor.
Another child barges in on a group game.	Let the other kids handle it.

Two rules are important to follow in making a plan of action with your child:

1. Don't accept any reason for fighting. The most common excuse I hear children give for fighting is that someone else started it. Self-defense is no excuse. Studies show that children who fight often mistake accidents for provocations.[4] Parents tell me their children stop fighting when they don't accept any excuse for fighting.

2. Don't allow your child to watch other children fighting. The other common excuse I hear children use is that they weren't involved in the fight; they were just watching or trying to break up a fight between other children. But breaking up the fight is a job for an adult. If you make this rule and then your child is anywhere near a fight, you know he is in the wrong. You don't have to ask a lot of questions, and it's easy to enforce.

John's mom teaches John to avoid fights:

MOM: Fighting is never acceptable. What will you do the next time George takes your ball?
JOHN: But it's my ball. He can't have it!
MOM: But fighting is wrong. What else will you do?
JOHN: I won't touch him. I'll just go away.

MOM: I'm glad you won't touch him. You don't have to go away, but don't do anything, and see how long he keeps it before he gets tired of having it. He is probably trying to get you angry.

JOHN: Okay.

This discussion with John will not be enough to stop fighting.

Step 4: Give an Immediate, Brief Penalty for Each Instance of Fighting

As in Chapter Twenty-Five, use these guidelines for the penalty:

1. The penalty should be brief, no longer than one or two hours.

2. The penalty should not be fun. There should be no games, TV, pleasant conversation, team sport, scout meeting, or anything else. If there is a movie you were planning on going to, it's canceled. If your child had a play date, make the penalty last until the play date (otherwise you're punishing the guest). If the play date starts too soon, give the penalty after the play date. Never use any kind of physical response that will cause your child pain as a penalty.

3. State the exact penalty before beginning it—for example, "I'm glad we came up with something better for you to try next time. But for now, no TV or games until 6:00 P.M."

4. After the penalty is over, do not discuss it further. Don't ask for an apology from your child.

Give this penalty every time your child gets in trouble, including the first time.

Step 5: Check Back with the Complaining Adult

Keep track of the number of incidents by getting daily or weekly reports from the complaining adult. If the number amounts to several each week, keep track of weekly totals.

Plan A
If weekly totals decrease, congratulations! Keep it up. You're on the right track!

Plan B
If weekly totals increase or stay the same for three weeks, seek professional help.[5]

• • •

I have summarized the steps to stop your child's fighting.

✓ Checklist for Stopping
Physical Fighting ✓

Step 1: Talk to the complaining adult.
- Be polite. Check if you are talking to the adult at a convenient time for him.
- Stay calm.
- Ask for specifics.
- Express your concern about the issue and your availability to work together with him or her.
- Arrange to keep communication open.

Step 2: When you get home, talk to your child about the troublesome incident.
- Don't accuse your child of being in the wrong. This will get you nowhere and make it difficult for your child to continue the conversation.
- Don't dispute your child's side of the story or say to your child, "Tell the truth." This will take you off-track, and you will never know the truth. What matters most is that your child doesn't repeat the offense.
- Don't lecture. Your child will tune you out after you say the first few words.

Step 3: Have your child think of better ways to handle the incident. There are two rules your child should follow in this situation:

- Don't accept any reason for fighting.
- Don't allow your child to watch other children fighting.

Step 4: Give an immediate, brief penalty after each instance of talking back.

1. The penalty should be brief, no longer than one or two hours. Never use any kind of physical response that will cause your child pain as a penalty.

2. Penalty time should not be fun. If your child had a play date, make the penalty last until the play date (otherwise you're also punishing your child's friend). If the play date will start too soon, give the penalty after the play date.

3. State the exact penalty before beginning it.

4. After the penalty is over, do not discuss it further. Wipe the slate clean.

Step 5: Check back with the complaining adult.

Plan A: If weekly totals decrease: Keep it up. You're on the right track!

Plan B: If weekly totals increase or stay the same: If this happens for three weeks, seek professional help.

The Next Step

Fighting is a difficult problem, and you deserve a lot of credit for seeing this through. Fighting not only interferes with friendships but sometimes leads to more serious problems in adolescence. If your child's fighting has damaged his reputation, read Chapter Thirty. Then you can go to the chapters in Parts Two and Three to get the help your child needs to make and keep friends.

27

Overcoming Hyperactive Behavior

———————•———————

The Problem

- My child constantly acts without thinking and quickly alienates playmates. What can I do?
- My child doesn't seem to be able to stick to playing games and activities like other children his age. What can I do?

Background: The Child with Attention-Deficit/ Hyperactivity Disorder

Eleven-year-old Gus gets C's and D's in school, despite seeming quite bright. He frequently calls out in class, and his messy schoolwork annoys his teacher.

He is friendly and outgoing with other boys, has a high energy level, and talks easily with anyone. But after boys know him for a while, he begins to get on their nerves. He is the first to point out when they are playing poorly, and he sometimes has trouble waiting his turn and will leave in the middle of a game.

Gus has attention-deficit/hyperactivity disorder (ADHD). Its major symptoms are:[1]

1. Often fails to give close attention to details or makes care-less mistakes in schoolwork or other activities

2. Often has difficulty sustaining attention in tasks or play activities

3. Often does not seem to listen when spoken to directly

4. Often does not follow through on instructions and fails to finish schoolwork or chores

5. Often has difficulty organizing tasks or activities

6. Often avoids, dislikes, or is reluctant to engage in tasks that require sustained mental effort (such as schoolwork or homework)

7. Often loses things necessary for tasks or activities

8. Often easily distracted by extraneous stimuli

9. Often forgetful in daily activities

And/or at least six of the following:

1. Often fidgets with hands or feet or squirms in seat

2. Often leaves seat in situations where remaining seated is expected

3. Often runs about or climbs excessively in situations in which it is inappropriate

4. Often has difficulty playing quietly

5. Often on the go or often acts as if driven by a motor

6. Often talks excessively

7. Often blurts out answers before questions have been completed

8. Often has difficulty waiting turn

9. Often interrupts or intrudes on others

ADHD has two major effects on Gus:

- It limits his ability to concentrate on activities, especially those that last for a long time and require sustained mental effort.

- It decreases his self-control. Gus can't take turns,
  barges into things without knowing what is going on,
  and alienates others with his impulsive behavior. He
  teases others without thinking and is teased in
  retaliation.

Studies show that about half of children with ADHD have difficulties making and keeping friends.[2] About 60 percent of them talk back to adults or fight with others (see Chapters Twenty-Five and Twenty-Six to deal with these problems).[3] Children with ADHD and friendship problems may find it especially hard to respect the rights of others during competitive games and stick with activities that require them to be seated (although they can get hooked on video games). These characteristics may make them poor playmates and teammates. Children with ADHD also may show poor judgment in their choice of playmates.

Some children with ADHD don't seem to have a natural talent for sports and seem to lack the persistence to learn to play a sport adequately. Other children with ADHD excel in sports but are hard to get along with because they constantly criticize their teammates or brag about winning. The child with ADHD may get yelled at and picked on by teammates and even coaches. He may show others that he is a poor sport. Instead of attracting friends, he may find that his teammates avoid him after games and practices.

Gus tries to join a group of toughs playing basketball. He doesn't try to figure out what they're playing and just barges in. He points out that one boy made a stupid move. He points out when another boy is out of bounds. The boys decide it would be more fun to pin him on the ground. Gus gets the message that he should not be in the game. When he gets home, he tells his dad what the boys did to him. His dad enrolls him in a karate class.

Poor impulse control makes activities like karate an especially poor choice for children like Gus. Rather than learning that he needs to defend himself after he's made a poor choice for playmates, he needs to learn how to avoid boys who fight, stay out of fights, choose playmates wisely, make a good first impression, and be a good sport.

Solving the Problem: Dealing with ADHD

Gus can learn the social skills that he needs, and his parents can take steps to deal with his ADHD and teach him the relationship skills he needs.

Step 1: Get a Proper Evaluation

If you suspect your child has ADHD, have your child evaluated by a child psychiatrist or pediatrician. Because ADHD affects a child's ability to concentrate for long periods of time, symptoms are often missed during a brief interview with the child. Currently the best way to diagnose ADHD is with an interview with you and check-lists given to both you and your child's teachers.

Step 2: Get Treatment If Your Child Needs It

Children with ADHD are as different from one another as any other children. Some children with ADHD have difficulty listen-ing to parents and teachers, do poorly in school, and have few or no friends, while others show few of these problems. The treat-ments most effective in meeting these needs are, in order of likely effectiveness, stimulant medication, parent training, and social skills training.

STIMULANT MEDICATION
Medicating a child is a difficult decision for parents, and there has been much serious discussion and controversy around this issue, with some professionals showing that children are overmedicated, medicated for the wrong reasons, and poorly followed up.[4] Some professionals have shown that stimulants can help under appropri-ate circumstances.[5] Complementary and alternative medicines are now receiving attention, with some evidence gathering for both their effectiveness and some potential side effects.[6]

If you have decided to pursue medication for your child, a child psychiatrist or pediatrician can determine if medication will help your child. Recently long-acting stimulants (those that last ten to twelve hours) have been developed. Stimulants can help the friendships of children with ADHD by strengthening their ability to attend to what other children are saying, sustain interest in playing games, and control impulses. Stimulants are best evaluated by having the child's teacher fill out checklists on days the child is on and off medication to see if the medication has the desired effect.

PARENT TRAINING

A professional helps teach you skills that will help your child obey you and his teachers better if these are problems.

SOCIAL SKILLS TRAINING

Your child is helped in a group of at least four other children to learn the social graces taught in this book. Research has shown that the approaches in this book can help children with ADHD.[7]

Step 3: Choose Play Activities That Match Your Child's Attention Span

Some children with ADHD can't pay attention to more complicated games or sports in which there is a lot of waiting, such as baseball and T-ball. In this case, my advice is to stick to simple games, choose soccer and basketball instead, and plan play experiences shorter than your child's attention span. For example, if your child cannot attend to activities longer than one hour, arrange for activities and play dates that last about forty-five minutes. If medication helps your child attend longer, talk to your prescribing physician about giving your child his medication before playing.

Step 4: Help Your Child Choose Playmates Wisely

Children with ADHD are usually one to two years behind other children their age in their understanding of social graces, even when they are intellectually bright. For this reason, it is okay to let them play with peers who are a year or so younger.

Children with ADHD are high energy and naturally gravitate together. This happens either by choice or out of desperation, after they find that no one else will play with them. Discourage friendships with other children with ADHD, however, because two children with this disorder are more difficult for parents to manage on play dates, and sometimes they lack a voice of reason and impulsively try dangerous and inappropriate activities.

Follow the steps in Chapters Fifteen and Sixteen to discourage a poor choice friendship.

Step 5: Manage Play Dates

Don't make play dates with other children with ADHD. Two children with ADHD playing together can be much less in control of themselves than either is alone.

Always make a play date for shorter periods than your child's attention span. If he gets tired of playing after two hours, make the play date for an hour and a half. It's easier to continue a play date that is going well than to cut short a play date that has gone sour. If your child's attention span is lengthened by stimulants, give medication before the play date is to start, but consult with your child's physician to ensure this is okay.

The Next Step

If you have sought professional help for your child, you have taken the first step in helping your child overcome problems caused by ADHD. Chapter Thirty will help you to repair your child's reputation among classmates before you go on to teaching your child new skills to make and keep friends (see the chapters in Parts One and Two).

28

Stopping Your Child's Bullying

———•———

The Problem

- How can I stop my child from being cruel to others?

Background: Common Patterns of Severe Bullying

The principal calls you in for a conference about your child and tells you that he and his friend have been taunting and scaring a younger girl. This is how parents most often discover their child has been bullying. Their child may be well liked and do well academically. All you knew up to this point was that your child had a circle of friends. Maybe you had doubts about some of these friends, but nothing serious enough for you to act on. In fact, there is no obvious profile for children who bully.

A boy bully is cruel to a specific child over a long period of time. Bullying groups usually have a leader who is physically stronger than most others his age. There are usually one or two followers; they don't lead attacks on others but enjoy watching them or help come up with new ideas. If the child being bullied is disliked by classmates, more children may join in the bullying group.

Your child's bullying is not a reflection on you, but an indication that

- Your child has nothing better to do with his time.
- He has fallen in with the wrong circle of friends.
- He needs to learn from you that it is always wrong to pick on others, even if no one else likes them.

Solving the Problem: How to Stop Bullying

Eliminate these reasons for bullying as follows.[1]

Step 1: Do Not Support Bullying

Nothing justifies bullying, even if the victim is disliked by most others. Give your child the clear message that what he did was wrong:

DAD: Your principal tells me that you've been bothering a younger girl every day at recess.

TYLER: She's always annoying the rest of the kids, and I don't really bother her.

DAD: You have no reason to be near a younger girl.

Step 2: Give Your Child Six Simple Rules to Prevent Bullying

Surgically remove that portion of your child's life that was devoted to bullying. If your child used a cell phone or computer to bully, take these away (or eliminate Internet access for the computer). If the school principal has complained to you about bullying, reassure her that you are taking action. Make sure that the school will also supervise your child. Simple rules need less detective work and are easily enforced. Here's what you tell your child:

1. Stay away from the child you picked on.

2. You are not allowed to hang out with the other kids who were bullying with you or had a part in cell phone or Internet harassment.

3. Go directly to school and come directly home from school. (These are prime times for bullying. You may have to enforce this by driving your child to and from school for a while.)

4. When you invite children over, play only on our property so that I know where you are at all times.

5. You are not allowed to visit someone else's house before I meet him and his parents. (In this case, you make sure that none of the friends he visits were part of the bullying group. Try to have other parents agree that he is not to have access to a cell phone or the Internet.)

6. When you go to someone else's house, you need to stay where his parent can see you at all times.

Here's how Dad tells these rules to Tyler:

DAD: From now on, the girl you were annoying is off-limits to you. You are not to be within twenty feet of her and are never to talk to her. Do you understand?

TYLER: That's not fair!

DAD: There's no excuse for bothering her.

TYLER: I don't bother her.

DAD: Then it should be easy for you to do what I said. Since the principal told me that Andy was doing this with you, you are not to play with Andy. Since this happened on the way to school, I will be driving you to school until you show us we can trust you again.

Children like Tyler will be quietly resigned to the restrictions after parents and teachers become involved. The actions of the adults make it clear that what he did was wrong. A soon-to-be former bully usually sees that what he did is wrong and that these restrictions are just. Dad has corrected a potential character flaw.

Step 3: Check on Your Child's Activities Outside Your Home

Before accepting an invitation for a play date, always tell the host's parent that one of your rules is that your child be supervised at all times (you don't have to say why). After the play date, always ask the host's parent about the activities of the play date. Here's how Tyler's mom questions Dylan's mom:

> MOM: Was Tyler okay?
> DYLAN'S MOM: He was okay.
> MOM: What did they do?
> DYLAN'S MOM: They shot some hoops out in the back yard.
> MOM: What else did they do?
> DYLAN'S MOM: They hung out in the tree house.
> MOM: That must have been fun.

If Dylan's mom didn't know what they were doing or let them go somewhere unsupervised, then steer Tyler away from Dylan.

Step 4: Provide an Immediate, Brief Penalty After One of the Rules Is Broken

Remember these guidelines:

1. Don't use any kind of physical response as a penalty. Remember that you're teaching that physical intimidation is never acceptable.

2. Don't restrict other aspects of your child's life. You want him to acquire more productive interests. Never take away a play date with another child who doesn't bully.

3. Select a penalty you can enforce. If your child has damaged another child's belongings, take away a week of his allowance to pay for part of it. It is not necessary for your child to totally repay the damage (although you offer to totally compensate the family of the injured child if property was taken or destroyed). Other appropriate penalties are restriction in TV time for the evening or missing a movie your child was planning to see.

4. Give the penalty immediately after you find out a rule has been broken.

5. State the exact penalty before beginning it—for example:

    > "Since you destroyed that child's backpack, I'll pay your allowance for the next week to him and I'll throw in my own money to make sure the backpack is replaced."

    > "Since I saw you standing next to Alan and you weren't supposed to go near him, there will be no TV tonight."

    > "You left the backyard when you were not supposed to. There will be no TV tonight."

6. After the penalty is over, do not discuss it further, and wipe the slate clean.

Step 5: Keep Track of Rule Violations

If your child frequently breaks the rules you have set up, continue to impose penalties, but consider seeking professional help.[2]

The Next Step

You deserve a lot of credit for dealing with your child's bullying. Children who bully have fallen in with the wrong crowd, and this crowd can sometimes lead them into more serious trouble as they get older. Read Chapters Fifteen and Sixteen to help your child select new friends to replace those who were bullying with him.

29

Not Noticed by Classmates

———•———

The Problem

- My child never wants to try what other children are playing. She usually goes off and stays by herself. What can I do to help?

Background: Children Who Hold Back

Some children without friends may have a lot to offer others but hold back and don't try to join others at play. These children have two things in common:

- Their behavior keeps them from being noticed by their classmates.
- Their behavior can be very frustrating for parents because they usually refuse to try anything new.

There are three related behavior patterns to look for: shy, worried, and sad. Although these behaviors have many differences, children who show them are all reluctant to try new things. Table 29.1 will help you determine if one of these patterns is keeping your child from being noticed.

Table 29.1 Behavior That Keeps Children from Being Noticed

Shy Behavior	Worried Behavior	Sad Behavior
Can't speak in public	Can't start new things	Can't get motivated
Doesn't approach new children	Constantly asks for reassurance	Had close friends but lost them
Waits for others to initiate friendship	Has to be "perfect" or is reluctant to participate	Has lost interest in most play activities
Doesn't know how to make friends	Is unable to relax	Is less energetic than age-mates
Is reluctant to try new things	Constantly struggles with you	Rarely smiles or shows pleasure
	Is reluctant to try new things	Is reluctant to try new things

Children Who Act Shy

Deborah, age eight, isolates herself from her classmates, although she is a chatterbox at home. It's the second month of school, and she has not said a word in her second-grade class. Initially the other girls asked if she wanted to join in. But she silently shook her head "no." She is not familiar with many of the games the other girls play, although she is one of the fastest runners of all the girls. They are busy having fun, so they soon give up and stop noticing her. She seems content to play by herself.

Deborah's quiet, cautious temperament is the main reason she acts shy. She also doesn't think that others will value what she has to say. She has always been slow to warm up to new situations, although as she grows older, this is much less true. Studies show that shy children know little about how to make friends.[1]

Children Who Are Worried

Fears and worries are a normal part of growing up for many children. Here are some common fears and the typical ages at which they occur:

Common Fear	Typical Age Range
Strangers	6–9 months old
Separation, being alone	1–3 years old
Dark, monsters	4–8 years old
Natural disasters, snakes and spiders, injury	8–12 years old

Studies report that up to 95 percent of children have at least one of these fears while growing up.[2] These fears do not usually interfere with friendships. Be concerned when your child's fears depart from this by being unusual, especially severe, long lasting, or interfering with activities that other children do at the same age. If any of these conditions applies, your child may have anxiety problems.

Katie is nine years old and afraid to go to sleep by herself. She adamantly refuses to go to other girls' houses for sleepovers. One time she tried to stay over at Evelyn's house for a birthday sleepover, but at ten o'clock that night, she telephoned her parents to pick her up. The other girls are getting to know each other well and forming friendship groups. Katie is missing out because of her fears.

Katie's parents need to judge whether Katie's fear is keeping her from continuing in a friendship group. Sleepovers are important for strengthening these friendships.

Chris, nine years old going on thirty, is a constant worrier according to his parents. When his gym teacher begins to instruct the class on a new game, Chris becomes agitated and fidgety. The child standing next to him hears him mutter, "I don't get it. The kids are going to make fun of me." Chris's worry about failure distracts him from listening to the rules of the game. When it comes time to start the game, Chris begins to cry and walk away.

Chris has to do things perfectly. He lets this worry spoil a game. He is constantly complaining about stomachaches, headaches, and other worries.

A common, but ineffective, approach that well-meaning parents use is to try to convince the worried child that there is nothing to worry about. But this approach only deepens the worry. A better choice is to get the worried child to try new things without trying to convince him first (worried children think too much and do too little). Telling them in detail about exactly what is to happen sometimes helps. As he does more things, he will worry less about doing them.

Children Who Are Sad

Many friendless children are lonely and sad because they have no one to play with. Their sadness disappears once they are taught how to make friends. Other friendless children have had friends in the past but don't now because they are overwhelmed with other problems.

William's fourth-grade teacher describes him as inattentive and quiet. Most of his classmates don't even know he's around. His mother has seen his grades slip slowly over the past three years from C's to D's. He has stomachaches whenever there is a test at school. Both parents notice that he is always tired and lacks the energy to do things, including playing with other children.

His father frequently picks on him, calling him lazy. William is his only son and is a disappointment to his father. When William's mom brings him in for a comprehensive evaluation at a mental health clinic, he reports thinking about killing himself. This surprises his mother because he never has said anything like that to her.

Sometimes children become sad for reasons that their parents don't understand. Sadness in children is very hard for adults to notice. Parents will feel their depressed mood is just part of the way they are ("He's not very energetic"). Teachers, who usually do notice children's problems, will not notice the sad child because sad children blend into the woodwork and don't cause any problems to others. William's parents and teacher misinterpreted his sadness as laziness and inattentiveness. Childhood should be a basically happy time. If it's not, then something is wrong.

A child who is sad can appear lethargic, cranky, or irritable most of the day. Other symptoms are significant weight loss or gain, trouble sleeping or sleeping too much, chronic fatigue, and trouble making decisions.

The sad child may admit to thinking about suicide. Take children who talk about killing themselves seriously if they also have some of the other symptoms I have mentioned. If your child appears sad, consult a mental health professional for an evaluation of your child's problems.[3]

Solving the Problem: Getting Your Child to Try New Activities

Shy, worried, or sad children don't want to do things. They're not sure they want to play baseball or learn how to swim. Parents I know who successfully manage a child with one of these problems teach the worried child to worry less and do more. Here's how.

Step 1: Pick an Easy Activity at First

Pick something easy for your child to try first. If your child is hesitant to go to camp, for example, try a two-hour class, working up to a day camp. If your child is hesitant to spend the whole night at someone's house, try a couple of hours at first (asking the host's parents if this is okay):

KATIE'S MOM: Thanks for inviting Katie over to Evelyn's sleepover. I'd really like her to go, but she says she's uncomfortable about sleeping at someone else's house.

EVELYN'S MOM: Oh, that's too bad.

KATIE'S MOM: Could she come for part of it? When she gets there, she might want to stay for the whole night, but I'd be glad to pick her up if she doesn't.

EVELYN'S MOM: That would be okay.

KATIE'S MOM: I really appreciate this. How late can I call to see if she needs me to pick her up?

EVELYN'S MOM: We go to bed at 11:00, so any time before then would be fine.

KATIE'S MOM: That would be great. Thanks a lot.

Step 2: Make a Pact

Chris's mom does not allow Chris to make the decision as to whether or not to start a new activity, since whatever the activity, the answer will be no. Instead she sets up a pact with Chris:

CHRIS: I don't want to go to scouts.

MOM: Why not?

CHRIS: Because it will be boring.

MOM: I want you to try it for the next two Mondays. If it's boring, you can tell me at the end of each day, and we'll think about doing something else.

Similarly, Katie's mom has her stay for part of the sleepover:

MOM: Do you want to go to Evelyn's sleepover?

KATIE: Yes, but I'm afraid to sleep by myself.

MOM: I think you can do it. I want you to try. I've talked to Evelyn's mom, and she says it's okay if I call at 10:30 and talk to you. You can tell me how things are going when I call.

KATIE: Call me at 10:00.

MOM: Okay. I'll call you at 10:00.

Step 3: Evaluate the Activity

When Chris's mom picks him up from scouts on Monday, she wants to find out if Chris enjoyed himself. She uses the listening techniques in Chapter Seventeen, so she waits a bit to see if Chris will say something about it. She knows he is most likely to talk about scouts while it is still fresh in his mind. She waits for him to start talking about it during the car ride home. If he doesn't, then she tries a couple of leading questions:

MOM: How was scouts today—interesting or boring?

CHRIS: It was interesting.

MOM: Good. We will do it again next week. That's when we will decide whether you will continue to attend.

If Chris likes scouts, she stops the appraisals. If Chris doesn't like scouts, then he stops attending.

Similarly, Katie's mom calls at 10:00. She asks Katie whether she's having fun and avoids questions about her fear.

PLAN A

If Katie says she'd like to come home, her mom picks her up and brings her back home, apologizing to Evelyn's mother. Here's how she handles this:

MOM: Are you having fun?

KATIE: Yes. But I'm still worried I might get scared later.

MOM: I'll come pick you up. Let me talk to Evelyn's mom.

EVELYN'S MOM: Hi. What's going on?

KATIE'S MOM: Katie's not sure she can stay tonight. I'd like to pick her up in about twenty minutes, if that's okay.

EVELYN'S MOM: That's fine.

KATIE'S MOM: I'm sorry to cause you so much trouble. Thanks for being so understanding.

Katie's mom picks her up and praises her for staying as long as she did.

PLAN B
If Katie says she'd like to stay, praise her for staying.

You may have to repeat steps 1 to 3 several times before your child becomes comfortable. If the problem continues for much longer, then perhaps it is time to seek professional help.[4]

The Next Step

It's hard for most parents to keep after their child to try new things, but you've done it: your child has tried new things. You also know the signs that indicate you should seek professional help for your child. There are many treatments that have strong evidence for their effectiveness, and your child will suffer less in the long run. You are now ready to go back to Parts One and Two to help your child make friends.

30

Building Friendship Skills and Overcoming a Negative Reputation

———————•———————

Friendships can be an integral part of our daily lives that we sometimes take for granted. Yet they can make the difference between a lonely and a richly rewarding life.

Friendships start on a basis of common interests: What are you going to do together when you get together? In order to have friends, you have to have interests to share with others, and you must not let competition interfere with friendships. Your first task when you meet someone new whom you like is to search for common ground interests. In order to do this and to get to know someone better, you have to be able to share a conversation. You moderate personal disclosure, starting off with superficial exchanges of information and testing the waters with slightly intimate disclosures. If these disclosures are reciprocated, you proceed to more intimate disclosures. In all likelihood, you have learned these skills during your childhood.

Friendship is a child's first experience with true love: putting someone on at least an equal footing with themselves. They see that concern for another, having a good time, and taking care of them add to the joy of the relationship. Children who have difficulty making and keeping friends can commit many errors along this path. I have learned much about these errors, how to help children with them and have devoted a chapter to each of these in this book. Children who are liked and accepted by others know how to try to join a game politely (Chapter Seven), how to be a good sport (Chapter Eight), how to handle teasing without teasing back (Chapter Twenty-One), and how to be a gracious host on a play date (Chapter Thirteen). Children who break these social rules have few or no friends and develop a negative reputation.

The best way to help the child with a negative reputation is to teach the child skills that will make him or her a better playmate. Much of this book has been devoted to changing your child's reputation with skills to make her more fun to play with. In order to be successful in teaching these skills, you should try the steps in the chapters as she meets new children who don't know her. Even if your child has developed good social skills, it will take a while for the other children who know her to catch on. Take any pressure off your child to be accepted by the children who are avoiding her until you teach her the skills she needs to have. If your child stops making social errors, eventually the other children will forget, and her negative reputation will die down.

Closing Thought

Learning is a lifelong pursuit. I hope you have learned something useful from this book and that I have helped you help your child embark on a path of intimate friendships. I have learned much from the people I have helped. I encourage you to write to me, care of the publisher, telling me what you have learned.

NOTES

---•---

Introduction

1. Asher, S. R. (1990). Recent advances in the study of peer rejection. In S. R. Asher & J. D. Coie (Eds.), *Peer rejection in childhood* (pp. 3–14). Cambridge: Cambridge University Press.

2. Hymel, S., LeMare, L., Rowden, L., & Rubin, K. H. (1990). Children's peer relationships: Longitudinal prediction of internalizing and externalizing problems from middle to late childhood. *Child Development, 61,* 2004–2021.

3. Bagwell, C. L., Newcomb, A. F., & Bukowski, W. M. (1998). Preadolescent friendship and peer rejection as predictors of adult adjustment. *Child Development, 69(1),* 140–153.

4. Hartup, W. W. (1996). The company they keep: Friendships and their developmental significance. *Child Development, 67,* 1–13.

5. Malik, N. M., & Furman, W. (1993). Practitioner review: Problems in children's peer relations: What can the clinician do? *Journal of Child Psychology and Psychiatry, 34,* 1303–1326.

6. U.S. Department of Education: see http://www.ed.gov/espanol/parents/academic/ciudadano/page_pg14.html?exp=2 and http://www.ed.gov/parents/academic/help/citizen/partx4.html.

7. PBS Kids: http://pbskids.org/itsmylife/parents/resources/friendsfight
   .html. Family First: http://www.familyfirst.net/famminute/
   transcripts/2005/trans08-24-2005.html.

8. Stultz, S. (1998). Book review. *Journal of Child and Adolescent
   Group Therapy*, 8, 155.

9. Adoptive families.com: http://www.adoptivefamilies.com/articles.
   php?aid=344. NLDLine: http://www.nldline.com/bibliography.htm.
   ADDAdvisor: http://www.addvisor.com/addvisorvol5no9.htm.
   International Nanny Association: http://www.nanny.org/
   educationalresources2.htm. The Child Anxiety Network: http://
   www.childanxiety.net/Resources_for_Parents.htm. Supporters and
   Advocates of Gifted Education: http://www.just-for-kids.com/
   SERSAGE.HTM.

10. Frankel, F., Myatt, R., & Cantwell, D. P. (1995). Training outpa-
    tient boys to conform with the social ecology of popular peers:
    Effects on parent and teacher ratings. *Journal of Clinical Child
    Psychology*, 24, 300–310. Frankel, F. (2005). Parent-assisted
    children's friendship training. In E. D. Hibbs & P. S. Jensen (Eds.),
    *Psychosocial treatments for child and adolescent disorders: Empirically
    based approaches* (2nd ed., pp. 693–715). Washington, DC:
    American Psychological Association.

11. Frankel, F., Myatt, R., Cantwell, D. P., & Feinberg, D. T. (1997).
    Parent assisted children's social skills training: Effects on children
    with and without attention-deficit hyperactivity disorder. *Journal of
    the Academy of Child and Adolescent Psychiatry*, 36, 1056–1064.

12. Frankel, F., Paley, B., Marquart, R., & O'Connor, M. J. (2006).
    Stimulants, neuroleptics and children's friendship training in
    children with fetal alcohol spectrum disorders. *Journal of Child and
    Adolescent Psychopharmacology*, 16(6), 777–789.

13. Frankel, F., & Myatt, R. (2007). Parent-assisted friendship training
    for children with autism spectrum disorders: Effects associated with
    psychotropic medication. *Child Psychiatry and Human Development*,
    37, 337–346.

14. Frankel, F., Myatt, R., Whitham, C., Gorospe, C. M., Sugar, C., &
    Laugeson, E. A. (in press). A randomized controlled study of

parent-assisted children's friendship training with children having autism spectrum disorders. *Journal of Autism and Developmental Disabilities*.

15. Frankel, F., Gorospe, C. M., Chang, Y., & Sugar, C. A. (2010). *Mothers' reports of play dates and observation of school playground behavior of children having high-functioning autism spectrum disorders*. Manuscript submitted for publication.

16. Frankel, F., & Myatt, R. (2002). *Children's friendship training*. New York: Brunner-Routledge.

17. Author unknown to me.

Part One

1. Gest, S. D., Sesma, A., Masten, A., & Tellegen, A. (2006). Childhood peer reputation as a predictor of competence and symptoms 10 years later. *Journal of Abnormal Child Psychology, 34*, 509–526.

Chapter One

1. Crespo, C. J., Smit, E., Troiano, R. P., Bartlet, S. J., Macera, C. A., & Andersen R. E. (2001). Television watching, energy intake, and obesity in US children: Results from the Third National Health and Nutrition Examination Survey, 1988–1994. *Archives of Pediatric and Adolescent Medicine, 155*, 360–365.

2. Andersen, R., Crespo, C., Bartlett, S., Cheskin, L., & Prat, M. (1998). Relationship of physical activity and TV watching with body weight and level of fatness among children: Results from the Third National Health and Nutrition Examination Survey. *JAMA, 279*, 938–942.

Chapter Two

1. Andersen, R., Crespo, C., Bartlett, S., Cheskin, L., & Pratt, M. (1998). Relationship of physical activity and TV watching with body weight and level of fatness among children: Results from the Third National Health and Nutrition Examination Survey. *JAMA, 279*, 938–942.

Chapter Three

1. Berndt, T. J., & Hoyle, S. G. (1985). Stability and change in childhood and adolescent friendships. *Developmental Psychology*, 1985, *21*, 1007–1015.

2. Clark, J., & Barber, B. L. (1994). Adolescents in postdivorce and always-married families: Self-esteem and perceptions of fathers' interest. *Journal of Marriage and the Family*, 56, 608–614.

3. Pettit, G. S., & Clawson, M. A. (1996). Pathways to interpersonal competence: Parenting and children's peer relations. In N. Vanzetti & S. Duck (Eds.), *A lifetime of relationships* (pp. 125–154). Monterey, CA: Brooks/Cole.

Chapter Four

1. Bryant, B. K. (1985). The neighborhood walk: Sources of support in middle childhood. *Monographs of the Society for Research in Child Development*, *50*(3), 1–22. Rubin, Z., & Sloman, J. (1984). How parents influence their children's friendships. In M. Lewis (Ed.), *Beyond the dyad* (pp. 223–250). New York: Plenum Press.

Chapter Five

1. Bryant, B. K. (1985). The neighborhood walk: Sources of support in middle childhood. *Monographs of the Society for Research in Child Development*, *50*(3), 1–22. Ladd, G. W., & Price, J. M. (1987). Predicting children's social and school adjustment following the transition from preschool to kindergarten. *Child Development*, 58, 1168–1189.

2. Orenstein, P. (1994). *Schoolgirls: Young women, self-esteem, and the confidence gap*. New York: Doubleday.

3. Kovacs, D. M., Parker, J. G., & Hoffman, L. W. (1996). Behavioral, affective, and social correlates of involvement in cross-sex friendship in elementary school. *Child Development*, 67, 2269–2286.

4. Morgan, B. L. (1998). A three generational study of tomboy behavior. *Sex Roles*, 39, 787–800.

5. Burn, S. M., O'Neil, A. K., & Nederland, S. (1996). Childhood tomboyism and adult androgyny. *Sex Role, 34,* 419–428.

6. Hyde, J. S., Rosenberg, B. G., & Behrman, J. A. (1977). Tomboyism. *Psychology of Women Quarterly, 2,* 73–75.

Chapter Seven

1. Garvey, C. *Children's talk.* (1984). Cambridge, MA: Harvard University Press.

2. Black, B., & Hazen, N. L. (1990). Social status and patterns of communication in acquainted and unacquainted preschool children. *Developmental Psychology, 26,* 379–387. Tryon, A. S., & Keane, S. P. (1991). Popular and aggressive boys' initial social interaction patterns in cooperative and competitive settings. *Journal of Abnormal Child Psychology, 19,* 395–406.

3. Dodge, K. A., Schlundt, D. C., Schocken, I., & Delugach, J. D. (1983). Social competence and children's sociometric status: The role of peer group entry strategies. *Merrill-Palmer Quarterly, 29,* 309–336.

4. Corsaro, W. A. (1981). Friendship in the nursery school: Social organization in a peer environment. In S. R. Asher & J. M. Gottman (Eds.), *The development of children's friendships* (pp. 207–241). Cambridge: Cambridge University Press.

Chapter Nine

1. Eder, D., & Hallinan, M. (1978). Sex differences in children's friendships. *American Sociological Review, 43,* 237–250.

2. Paxton, S. J., Schutz, H. K., Wertheim, E. H., & Muir, S. L. (1999). Friendship clique and peer influences on body image concerns, dietary restraint, extreme weight-loss behaviors, and binge eating in adolescent girls. *Journal of Abnormal Behavior, 108,* 255–266.

3. Adler, P. A., & Adler, P. (1995). The dynamics of inclusion and exclusion in preadolescent cliques. *Social Psychology Quarterly, 58,* 145–162.

4. Paxton et al. (1999).

Chapter Ten

1. Gottman, J. M. (1983). How children become friends. *Monographs of the Society for Research in Child Development, 48*(3), 1–85.

Chapter Eleven

1. Thurlow, C., & McKay, S. (2003). Profiling "new" communication technologies in adolescence. *Journal of Language and Social Psychology, 22*, 94–103. Bryant, J. A., Sanders-Jackson, A., & Smallwood, A.M.K. (2006). IMing, text messaging, and adolescent social networks. *Journal of Computer-Mediated Communication, 11*(2), article 10. Available at http://jcmc.indiana.edu/vol11/issue2/bryant.html.

2. Gross, E. F. (2004). Adolescent Internet use: What we expect, what teens report. *Journal of Applied Developmental Psychology, 25*, 633–649.

3. Comprehensive IM acronym dictionaries can be found at: http://www.aim.com/acronyms.adp and http://www.netlingo.com/acronyms.php.

Chapter Twelve

1. Bagwell, C. L., Newcomb, A. F., & Bukowski, W. M. (1998). Preadolescent friendship and peer rejection as predictors of adult adjustment. *Child Development, 69*, 140–153.

Chapter Thirteen

1. Gottman, J. M. (1983). How children become friends. *Monographs of the Society for Research in Child Development, 48*(3), 1–85.

Chapter Fifteen

1. Orenstein, P. (1994). *Schoolgirls: Young women, self-esteem, and the confidence gap.* New York: Doubleday.

Chapter Sixteen

1. Parkhurst, J. T., & Hopmeyer, A. (1998). Sociometric popularity and peer-perceived popularity: Two distinct dimensions of peer

status. *Journal of Early Adolescence, 18*, 125–144. Adler, P. A., & Adler, P. (1995). The dynamics of inclusion and exclusion in preadolescent cliques. *Social Psychology Quarterly, 58*, 145–162.

2. American Psychiatric Association. (2002). *Diagnostic and statistical manual of mental disorders* (4th ed., text rev.). Washington, DC: Author.

3. Hartup, W.W. (1993). Adolescents and their friends. In B. Laursen (Ed.), *Close friendships in adolescence*. New Directions for Child Development (W. Damon, series editor-in-chief), Number 60, 3–22.

4. Sourander, A., Elonheimo, H., Niemelä, S., Nuutila, A., Helenius, H., Sillanmäki, L., et al. (2006). Childhood predictors of male criminality: A prospective population-based follow-up study from age 8 to late adolescence. *Journal of the American Academy of Child and Adolescent Psychiatry, 45*, 578–586.

5. Mrug, S., Hoza, B., & Bukowski, W. M. (2004). Choosing or being chosen by aggressive-disruptive peers: Do they contribute to children's externalizing and internalizing problems? *Journal of Abnormal Child Psychology, 32*, 53–65.

6. Parker, J. G., & Asher, S. R. (1993). Friendship and friendship quality in middle childhood: Links with peer group acceptance and feelings of loneliness and social dissatisfaction. *Developmental Psychology, 29*, 611–621.

Chapter Eighteen

1. Crick, N. R., & Grotpeter, J. K. (1995). Relational aggression, gender, and social-psychological adjustment. *Child Development, 66*, 710–722.

2. Nelson, J., & Aboud, F. E. (1985). The resolution of social conflict between friends. *Child Development, 56*, 1009–1017.

Chapter Twenty

1. Wasserstein, S. B., & La Greca, A. M. (1996). Can peer support buffer against behavioral consequences of parental discord? *Journal of Clinical Child Psychology, 25*, 177–182.

Chapter Twenty-One

1. Perry, D. G., Kusel, S. J., & Perry, L. C. (1988). Victims of peer aggression. *Developmental Psychology, 26,* 807–814.

2. Salmivalli, C., & Nieminen, E. (2002). Proactive and reactive aggression among school bullies, victims, and bully-victims. *Aggressive Behavior, 28,* 230–244.

3. Warm, T. R. (1997). The role of teasing in development and vice versa. *Journal of Developmental and Behavioral Pediatrics, 18,* 97–101.

4. Perry, D. G., Williard, J. C., & Perry, L. C. (1990). Peers' perceptions of the consequences that victimized children provide aggressors. *Child Development, 61,* 1310–1325.

5. Scambler, D. J., Harris, M. J., & Milich, R. (1998). Sticks and stones: Evaluations of response to childhood teasing. *Social Development, 7,* 234–249.

Chapter Twenty-Two

1. Baumeister, R. F., Zhang, L., & Vohs, K. D. (2004). Gossip as cultural learning. *Review of General Psychology, 8,* 111–121.

2. Kuttler, A. F., Parker, J. G., & La Greca, A. M. (2002). Developmental and gender differences in preadolescents' judgments of the veracity of gossip. *Merrill-Palmer Quarterly, 48,* 105–132.

3. Bordia, P., DiFonzo, N., Haines, R., & Chaseling, E. (2005). Rumor denials as persuasive messages: Effects of personal relevance, source, and message characteristics. *Journal of Applied Social Psychology, 35,* 1301–1331.

4. Rosnow, R. L. (1988). Rumor as communication: A contextualist approach. *Journal of Communication, 38,* 12–28.

Chapter Twenty-Four

1. Olweus, D. (1993). *Bullying at school: What we know and what we can do.* Cambridge, MA: Blackwell.

2. Kipling, A. S., & Williams, D. (2004). R U There? Ostracism by cell phone text messages. *Group Dynamics: Theory, Research, and Practice, 8*, 291–301.

3. Beale, A. V., & Hall, K. R. (2007). Cyberbullying: What school administrators (and parents) can do. *Clearing House, 81*, 8–12.

Chapter Twenty-Five

1. A panel of psychologists has set up the following Web site to provide guidance in this area: http://www.effectivechildtherapy.com/.

Chapter Twenty-Six

1. Schwartz, D., Dodge, K. A., Pettit, G. S., & Bates, J. E. (1997). The early socialization of aggressive victims of bullying. *Child Development, 68*, 665–675.

2. A brief review is in Frankel, F., Myatt, R., & Cantwell, D. P. (1995). Training outpatient boys to conform with the social ecology of popular peers: Effects on parent and teacher ratings. *Journal of Clinical Child Psychology, 24*, 300–310.

3. American Psychiatric Association. (2002). *Diagnostic and statistical manual of mental disorders* (4th ed., text rev.). Washington, DC: Author.

4. Dodge, K. A. (1985). Attributional biases in aggressive children. In P. D. Kendall (Ed.), *Advances in cognitive-behavioral research and therapy* (Vol. 4, pp. 73–110). Orlando, FL: Academic Press.

5. A panel of psychologists has set up the following Web site to provide guidance in this area: http://www.effectivechildtherapy.com/.

Chapter Twenty-Seven

1. American Psychiatric Association. (2002). *Diagnostic and statistical manual of mental disorders* (4th ed., text rev.). Washington, DC: Author.

2. Frederick, B. P., & Olmi, D. J. (1994). Children with attention-deficit/hyperactivity disorder: A review of the literature on social skills deficits. *School Psychology Review, 31*, 288–296.

3. Jensen, P. S., Martin, D., & Cantwell, D. P. (1997). Comorbidity in ADHD: Implications for research, practice and DSM-V. *Journal of the Academy of Child and Adolescent Psychiatry, 36,* 1065–1079.

4. Rappley, M. D., Eneli, I. U., Mullen, P. B., Alvarez, F. J., Wang, J., Luo, Z., et al. (2002). Patterns of psychotropic medication use in very young children with attention-deficit hyperactivity disorder. *Developmental and Behavioral Pediatrics, 23,* 23–30. Sparks, J. A., & Duncan, B. L. (2004). The ethics and science of medicating children. *Ethical Human Psychology and Psychiatry, 6,* 25–39.

5. Jensen, P. S., Kettle, L., Roper, M. T., Sloan, M. T., Dulcan, M. K., Hoven, C., et al. (1999). Are stimulants overprescribed? Treatment of ADHD in four U.S. communities. *Journal of the American Academy of Child and Adolescent Psychiatry, 38,* 797–804. Kempton, S., Vance, A., Maruff, P., Luk, E., Costin, J., & Pantelis, C. (1999). Executive function and attention deficit hyperactivity disorder: Stimulant medication and better executive function performance in children. *Psychological Medicine, 20,* 527–538.

6. Chan, E. (2002). The role of complementary and alternative medicine in attention-deficit hyperactivity disorder. *Developmental and Behavioral Pediatrics, 23,* S37–S45.

7. Frankel, F., Myatt, R., Cantwell, D. P., & Feinberg, D.T. (1997). Parent assisted children's social skills training: Effects on children with and without attention-deficit hyperactivity disorder. *Journal of the Academy of Child and Adolescent Psychiatry, 36,* 1056–1064.

Chapter Twenty-Eight

1. Much of the approach of this chapter is adapted from Olweus, D. (1997). Bully/victim problems in school: Knowledge base and an effective intervention program. *Irish Journal of Psychology, 18,* 170–190.

2. A panel of psychologists has set up the following Web site to provide guidance in this area: http://www.effectivechildtherapy .com/.

Chapter Twenty-Nine

1. Fordham, K., & Stevenson-Hinde, J. (1999). Shyness, friendship quality, and adjustment during middle childhood. *Journal of Child Psychology and Psychiatry, 40,* 757–768.

2. Derevensky, J. L. (1979). Children's fears: A developmental comparison of normal and exceptional children. *Journal of Genetic Psychology, 135,* 11–21.

3. A panel of psychologists has set up the following Web site to provide guidance in this area: http://www.effectivechildtherapy.com/.

4. See note 3.

RESOURCES

———•———

This section lists some recommended readings based on research evidence and some movies. Most are older works, but they still offer the best examples in their categories. They remain in print at the time of this writing.

Books and Web Sites

Adoption

MacLeod, J., & Macrae, S. (2006). *Adoption parenting: Creating a toolbox, building connections*. Warren, NJ: EMK Press. Focuses on the task of adoption parenting. It provides a wealth of contacts to other adoption resources (books, Web sites, magazines, experts, mailing groups). The topics include sleep, food issues, learning difficulties, discipline, language development, and racism.

Adoptive Families, http://www.adoptivefamilies.com. A comprehensive adoption information source for families before, during, and after adoption.

Anxiety

Manassis, K. (1996). *Keys to parenting an anxious child*. Happauge, NY: Barron's. A good description of anxiety with easy-to-follow parenting steps. The book discusses how parenting style influences anxiety in children and how to communicate your child's problems to teachers and others working with your child.

Rapee, R., Wignall, A., Spence, S., Cobham, V., & Lyneham, H. (2008). *Helping your anxious child: A step-by-step guide for parents.* Oakland, CA: New Harbinger. For parents of children eight and older with helpful and clearly explained practical suggestions to help your child manage anxiety. Explains the links among thoughts, feelings, and anxiety.

Anxiety Disorders Association of America, http://www.adaa.org/. An anxiety disorders site put together by professionals with links to resources, therapists, and research studies across the Untied States.

Child Anxiety Network, http://www.childanxiety.net/index.htm. A helpful child anxiety disorders Web site with links to useful resources for professionals, parents, and children.

Asperger's Syndrome, Nonverbal Learning Disability, and High-Functioning Autism

Ozonoff, S., Dawson, G., & McPartland, J. (2002). *A parent's guide to Asperger syndrome and high-functioning autism: How to meet the challenges and help your child thrive.* New York: Guilford Press. Discusses diagnosis, treatments, dealing with home and school, and the social world of older persons with Asperger's syndrome and high-functioning autism. Included are numerous instances of older children in social situations such as dating, school, living on their own, and employment. The authors review general intervention strategies.

Autism Speaks, http://www.autismspeaks.org/about_us.php. The nation's largest autism science and advocacy organization, dedicated to funding research into the causes, prevention, and treatments for autism. It also aims to increase awareness of autism spectrum disorders and advocates for the needs of individuals with autism and their families.

Wing, L. (2001). *The autistic spectrum: A parents' guide to understanding and helping your child.* Berkeley, CA: Ulysses Press. Written by an internationally known authority in the field and the author of some landmark studies on autism, Wing is also the mother of an autistic child and world-renowned author of research in autism. She blends clinical knowledge with practical guidance. The amount of information can be overwhelming to parents.

Attention-Deficit/Hyperactivity Disorder

Barkely, R. A. (2000). *Taking charge of ADHD: The complete, authoritative guide for parents* (rev. ed.). New York: Guilford Press. Although it could be more user friendly because it employs technical jargon, this is a complete ADHD-related parenting book. It thoroughly reviews the scientific literature related to ADHD and describes scientifically supported treatments.

Hallowell, E. M., & Ratey, J. J. (1995). *Driven to distraction: Recognizing and coping with attention deficit disorder from childhood through adulthood.* New York: Touchstone. Written by two people who have ADHD themselves, they dispel a variety of myths about ADHD. They paint a concrete picture of the syndrome's realities and offer some helpful tips for dealing with a child with ADHD.

CHADD, http://www.chadd.org/. CHADD is a nonprofit organization founded by parents for education, advocacy, and support for children and adults with ADHD. It is a comprehensive site for local and national resources.

Bullying

Olweus, D. (1993). *Bullying at school: What we know and what we can do.* Cambridge, MA: Blackwell. Clearly presents facts about bullying, its causes and consequences, as well as the author's historic large-scale intervention study. It is based on a scientifically evaluated intervention program that produced a reduction of bullying by 50 percent. It contains practical advice to school principals, teachers, and parents on how to implement this program.

SAMHSA's National Mental Health Association Center, http://mentalhealth. samhsa.gov/15plus/aboutbullying.asp. A comprehensive site for parents and teachers to implement steps to prevent, recognize, and deter bullying.

Stop Bullying Now, http://www.stopbullyingnow.hrsa.gov/kids/. An interactive site mainly oriented toward children with things they can do about being bullied or witnessing someone else being bullied.

Depression

Seligman, M. E. (2007). *The optimistic child: Proven program to safeguard children from depression and build lifelong resilience.* New York: Houghton Mifflin. Written in an easy-to-understand manner, it presents optimism as a skill that can be taught to even those who are naturally pessimistic. Teaching children this skill can help them better avoid being overcome by depression.

National Institute of Mental Health, http://www.nimh.nih.gov/health/topics/ depression/depression-in-children-and-adolescents.shtml. Presents the latest research on depression and many resources for information and treatment.

Divorce

Long, N., & Forehand, R. (2002). *Making divorce easier on your child: 50 effective ways to help children adjust.* New York: McGraw-Hill. Easy-to-follow advice based on the authors' years of clinical experience dealing with the children of divorce, as well as their extensive research into the causes and cures of divorce-related emotional problems.

Medication

Wilens, T. (2008). *Straight talk about psychiatric medications for kids* (rev. ed.). New York: Guilford Press. Explains which medications are prescribed for children and why; their effects on health, emotions, and school performance; how to maximize the benefits; and when to consider other treatments. This book helps parents to find out what is wrong with their child and get a diagnosis and the most effective treatment.

Family Education, http://school.familyeducation.com/add-and-adhd/decision-making/34400.html?detoured=1. A comprehensive site that gives both sides of major issues facing parents of children with attention-deficit/hyperactivity disorder.

Overweight

Satter, E. (2000). *Child of mine: Feeding with love and good sense* (3rd ed.). Boulder, CO: Bull Publishing. Nutritionist Ellyn Satter's useful guide to taking the power struggle out of eating behavior and how to set things up so your child can regulate her food intake. Satter's philosophy is that it is the parents' job to determine what food gets offered and when, and it is the child's job to determine if he will eat the food and how much.

National Heart Lung and Blood Institute, http://www.nhlbi.nih.gov/health/public/heart/index.htm#obesity. Provides helpful tools for eating healthier and getting more active.

Parenting

Kazdin, A. E. (2008). *The Kazdin methods for parenting the defiant child with no pills, no therapy, no contest of wills.* New York: Mariner Books. A parent-friendly description of parenting techniques Dr. Kazdin has demonstrated to be effective with young children.

Common Sense Media, http://www.commonsensemedia.org/movie-reviews. Movie ratings geared toward parents of young children. Rates every factor parents want to know about.

Video Game Revolution, http://www.pbs.org/kcts/videogamerevolution/impact/
esrb.html. The PBS guide to children's video games.

Movies

These are some movies that have made an impression on me:

Adam. (2009). About a young adult with Asperger's syndrome and the
problems this order creates for adult relationships.

Made in China: The Story of Adopted Children from China. (2000). A TV movie
that tells the stories of children adopted from China living in a visibly
adoptive family.

Mean Girls. (2004). Offers many insights into the social structure of cliques
that many girls find in middle and high school.

Medicating Kids. (2001). *Frontline* examines the dramatic increase in the
prescription of behavior-modifying drugs for children. Available at
http://www.pbs.org/wgbh/pages/frontline/shows/medicating/.

Rain Man. (1988). A classic and realistic portrayal of an autistic savant who is
not capable of living on his own.

ABOUT THE AUTHOR

———●———

Fred Frankel is director of the world-renowned Parenting and Children's Friendship Programs at the University of California, Los Angeles (UCLA), and a leading expert on children's and teens' friendship skills. He is professor of medical psychology at UCLA, where he researches friendship treatment and teaches and trains pediatricians, psychologists, social workers, and child psychiatrists. He is the author of *Children's Friendship Training* and *Social Skills for Teenagers with Developmental and Autism Spectrum Disorders: The PEERS Treatment Manual*. Both are comprehensive manuals to help therapists treat children and teens with friendship problems.

INDEX

Page references followed by *t* indicate a table.

A

Acronyms for texting, 103
Activities: ADHD and matching
appropriate, 251; day camps,
144–145, 147–150; drop those that
don't yield friendships, 6–7; drop
those that soak up your time, 7–10;
finding friends through organized,
31–41; four basic rules for first time
in, 35–37; getting your child to try
new, 263–266; interfering with
friendships, 11–13; making car pool
work for you, 9–10; networking
opportunities at, 44–48; safety
issues of, 33–34, 101, 103–107;
sleepover camps, 145–146. *See also*
Groups; Interests; Play dates
Addiction to media, 12–13
ADHD (attention-deficit/
hyperactivity disorder): carefully
choosing playmates for children
with, 251–252; choosing play
activities matching attention span
of, 251; day camps for children
with, 147; getting appropriate
treatment for, 250–251; getting a
proper evaluation, 250; symptoms
and impact of, 247–250

ADHD treatments: parent training,
251; social skills training, 251;
stimulant medication, 250–251
Adult supervision: characteristics of
good/poor, 38; checking back with
complaining, 236–237, 244–245;
children who challenge, 229–238;
complaints about your child's
fighting by, 240–245; evaluating
neighborhood activity/play date,
37–39, 256; stopping rumors by
speaking with, 207–208. *See also*
Teachers
After-school play programs, 34
Age differences: for child making play
date arrangements, 95–96; in close
friendships, 80*t*–82; common fears
by, 261; conflict resolution
approaches and, 133*t*
Answering machine messages, 89–92
Antisocial interests, 162–163
Arguments: age differences and
approach to, 133*t*; avoiding play
date conflict and, 126–142; good
sportsmanship to avoid, 67–77;
when parent should step in to
settle, 136–137. *See also* Fighters/
fighting

Asperger's disorder, 163
Autism spectrum disorders, 147, 163

B

Balls, 22
Behavior rules: on avoiding fighters,
214; for avoiding problems with
adult supervisors, 234–235; for being
a good play date host, 116–117, 128–
135; for first time activity, 35–37; of a
good host, 128–130; of a good sport,
69–71; for joining other children at
play, 51–52, 53t; for nonaggressive
responses to provocations, 242–243;
to prevent bullying by your child,
254–257. See also Conflict
avoidance; Etiquette rules
Behavioral problem solutions: check
back with the complaining adult,
236–237, 244–245; checklist for
working with adults on, 237–238;
for fighting by your child, 239–246;
getting your child to try new
activities, 263–266; give immediate,
brief penalty for incidents, 235–236,
244; help your child use rules
facilitating, 234–235; how to stop
your child's bullying, 254–257; talk
to the complaining adult, 231–233;
talk to your child about the
situation, 233–234
Behavioral problems: ADHD
(attention-deficit/hyperactivity
disorder), 147, 247–252; Asperger's
disorder, 163; autism spectrum
disorders, 147, 163; avoiding
children with poor values/antisocial
interests, 162–163; avoiding poorly
behaved children, 161–162;
avoiding relationship with child
with serious, 163; behaviors
keeping children from being
noticed, 259–263; handling adult
complaints about your child, 229–
231; relational aggression, 175–179.
See also Bullying; Children; Social
world problems

Best friends: age differences in close
friendships and, 80t–82; gender
differences in, 181; handling
stolen, 175–179; helping your
child develop relationship with,
82–85; loss of a, 181–184.
See also Friends
Board games, 22
Body language, 170, 178
Boredom fix-it strategies, 129t
Boys: age differences in close
friendships, 80t–82; average
number of close friends of, 181;
how they join others at play, 53t.
See also Gender differences
Bullies: considering professional help
for your child, 257; hanging out
with friends to discourage, 224–
225; learning to disobey orders
from, 220–221; neutralizing the,
219–225; protecting the victim
from, 224; stopping your child
from being a, 253–257; taking
charge and doing the tattling on,
222–224
Bullying: characteristics of fighters
versus, 211–212t; common patterns
of severe, 253–254; cyberbullying
form of, 218–219; do not support
or justify, 254; friends who engage
in, 162–163; get as much detail
about the situation, 219–222;
getting information from teacher
about, 173–174; how to tell if you
child is suffering, 217–219;
immediate, brief penalty for, 256–
257; learning about your child's
exposure to, 170–174; progression
to severe, 217–218; relational
aggression in stealing friends as,
176–179; signs in your child's
behavior indicating, 218; six simple
rules to prevent, 254–257; staying
away from children engaging in,
211–225. See also Behavioral
problems; Classmates; Social world
problems; Teasing

C

Camps: children with special needs and, 146–147; day, 144–145, 147–150; sleepover, 145–146

Car pools: making them work for your child, 9–10; tips on forming, 10

Cell phones: cyberbullying using, 218–219; monitoring your child's use of, 107; safety reasons to have, 101; setting rules for using, 104–105; texting from, 101–103. *See also* Telephone use

Checkers game, 22

Checklists: basic play date, 122–123; complete play date, 139–142; good sport sessions, 76–77; joining neighborhood organized activities, 40–41; joining other children at play, 64–65; stopping physical fighting, 245–246; trading information on the telephone, 98–99; working with adults who have trouble with your child, 237–238

Chess, 22

Children: being a good host, 116–117, 125–142; building friendship skills of your, 267–268; encouraging them to try new activity, 34–35; fighting, 211–216, 239–246; joining others at play, 51–65; listening to your, 170–174; not noticed by classmates, 259–266; overscheduled, 6t–7; play date arrangements role by, 88t; with poor values or antisocial interests, 162–163; siblings of, 114–115; teaching them effective use of telephone, 87–99; who challenge adults, 229–238. *See also* Behavioral problems

Children with special needs: ADHD and, 147, 247–252; Asperger's disorder, 163; autism spectrum disorders, 147, 163; day camps for, 146–147

Chutes and Ladders, 22

Classes: children challenges adults in, 229–238; friendship benefits of neighborhood, 33

Classmates: contacting parents of your, 29–30; good and poor reasons to pick friends from, 29; stopping rumors spread by, 205–209; teasing by, 195–203; your child is not noticed by, 259–266. *See also* Bullying; Neighborhood schools

Close friendships: age differences in, 80t–82; arrange play dates with one child at a time to develop, 85; ask your child about favored playmates to develop, 83–84; linger to watch who your child interacts with, 84–85; loss of, 181–184; stolen friends situation threatening, 175–179

Clue Junior, 22

Coaches: cautiously involving yourself in activity with, 39; evaluating adult supervision of, 37–39

Communication: body language, 170, 178; direct approach to, 170–172; eye contact, 170, 178; voice tone, 171, 178; of your disapproval of bullying, 254. *See also* Listening to child

Computers: average time spent per week on, 3–4; cyberbullying using, 218–219; monitoring your child's use of, 107; setting rules for using, 104–105; spyware blocking/content filtering for, 103–104. *See also* Internet

Conflict avoidance: checklist for play date, 139–142; following the play date, 137–138; good sportsmanship for, 67–77; during play date, 131–132, 134–137; play date preparations for, 126–131; polite ways of, 130t. *See also* Behavior rules; Etiquette rules; Fighters/fighting

Conflict resolution: age differences and approach to, 133t; when parent should step in for, 136–137

Cub Scouts: encouraging your child to join, 264–265; example of when to drop, 8–9; how to join, 34; Pinewood Derby of, 67; sleepover camps run by the, 146; time commitment of, 6t
Cyberbullying, 218–219

D

Day camps: basic information on, 144–145; choosing the right one, 147–148; daily follow-up with your child on, 149–150; getting your child to try, 148–149; planning vacation play dates around the, 148
DeBaryshe, B. D., 212
Depression. *See* Sad behavior
Disclosure of information, 89
Divorce: helping child adjust to moving away after, 188–192; helping child maintain support of friends after, 187–188; helping your child adjust to changes of, 187–192; moving away due to, 185–187
Don't Break the Ice, 22
Dropping activities: that don't yield friendships, 6–7; that soak up your time, 7–10
Dungeons & Dragons, 22

E

E-mail blocks, 219
Electronic media: as addiction interfering with friendships, 11–12; average time spent per week on, 3–4; cell phones, 101–105, 107, 218–219; computer use, 3–4, 103–105, 107, 218–219; cyberbullying through, 218–219; negotiating deals over use of, 15–16; removing easy access to, 14; setting a reasonable weekly schedule of, 14–15. *See also* Technology
Emotional support, 44

Etiquette rules: for cell phone use, 104; for computer use, 104–105; on how to use the telephone, 92–93; IM (instant messaging) and texting, 105–106; for joining other children at play, 51–52, 53t. *See also* Behavior rules; Conflict avoidance
Eye contact, 170, 178

F

Fears: getting your child to try new activities and overcome, 263–266; sad behavior patterns related to, 259–260t, 262–263; shy behavior patterns related to, 259–260t; typical age range for, 261; worried behavior patterns related to, 259–260t, 261–262
Fighters/fighting: characteristics of children who are, 211–212t; checklist for stopping physical, 245–246; common excuses for, 243; follow-up discussion on avoiding the, 215–216; get the details from your child on the, 213–214; helping your child find nonaggressive alternatives to, 240–245; immediate, brief penalty for each instance of, 244; teaching your child to avoid the, 214–215; when your child is a, 239–240. *See also* Arguments; Conflict avoidance
First impressions: challenges of making good, 51; rules of etiquette for, 51–52, 53t; rules of a good sport to make good, 69–71. *See also* Joining other children
Freeing up time: calculating time your child has for close friends, 5; drop activities that don't yield friendships, 6–7; prime times for play dates, 5t

Friends: age differences in developing close, 80t; be firm about not reinviting poor choice for, 166–167; developing best, 87–99; discouraging poor choices in, 159–167; discussing the poorly chosen, 163–164; encouraging wise choices in, 153–158; friendship groups for developing close, 82–85; handling stolen, 175–179; learning about reputations of your child's, 156–157; make a pact about poorly chosen, 164–166; moving and making new, 191–192; moving and saying good-bye to, 188–189; neighborhood school classmates as, 27–30; talking to your child's, 155–156. See also Best friends

Friends of convenience: dropping time spent with, 6–7; one-sided friendships and, 160–161

Friendship choices: for children with ADHD, 251–252; five common types to voice, 159–163; guiding your child in making wise, 153–154; praise your child for making wise, 157–158; strategies for discouraging poor, 163–167; talk to your child about other children's reputations, 156–157; talk to your child's friends, 155–156

Friendship groups: avoiding the "popular kids" labeled, 82; developing interests that help form, 19–26; finding close friends through, 82–85; gender differences in patterns of, 181; girls' slow progression toward, 20; value of, 79, 81–82. See also Groups; Play dates

Friendship traps: children with behavioral problems, 163; children with poor values or antisocial interests, 162–163; one-sided friendships, 160–161; poorly behaved children, 161–162; the popular child, 159–160

Friendships: age differences in close, 80t–82; building your child's skills for, 267–268; developing best friend or close, 87–99; discouraging poor choices in, 159–167; dropping activities that don't yield, 6–7; encouraging wise choices in, 153–158; gender issues and, 32; interests that interfere with, 11–13; loss of close, 181–184; one-sided, 160–161; stolen friends situation threatening, 175–179; telephone as tool in developing, 87–89

Friendships cooling down: catching things at the early stage, 183; help your child grieve for lost friend, 184; scheduling play dates with others to cope with, 183–184; three stages of, 182–183; two common reasons for, 181–182

G

Games: becoming a good sport, 67–77; don't let your child prematurely end, 74; teaching child to join, 51–65. See also Neighborhood activities

Gender differences: close friendship development and, 80t–82; eye contact and, 170; joining others at play, 53t; neighborhood activities and, 32; in number of close friends/friendship groups, 181; in use of telephone with friends, 80t. See also Boys; Girls

Get-togethers. See Play dates

Girls: age differences in close friendships, 80t–82; average number of close friends of, 181; benefits of "girls only" activities for, 32; how they join others at play, 53t; relational aggression among, 175–179; self-identified tomboys, 32. See also Gender differences

Golf camp, 145

Good sportsmanship: checklist for teaching, 76–77; how winning at all costs differs from, 68t; importance of teaching children, 67–68; teaching your child, 68–77

Good sportsmanship sessions: bring an icebreaker toy, 69; don't let your child prematurely end the game, 74; encourage your child to attempt to join, 71; make pact with child before next, 74–75; praise your child for being a good sport, 74; see that your child follows the rules, 71–73; teach the rules of a good sport, 69–71

Good supervisor qualities, 38

Groups: Cub Scouts, 6t, 8–9, 34, 67, 146, 264–265; friendship benefits of neighborhood, 33. *See also* Activities; Friendship groups

Guests. *See* Play date guests

H

Helpful support, 44

Hopscotch, 22

Hosts. *See* Play date hosts

Humorous comebacks, 200–203

I

Icebreaker toys, 69

IM (instant messaging): blocking, 106–107; cyberbullying using, 218–219; example of typical, 102; helping your child choose a screen name for, 105; moving away and staying in touch through, 191; play date arrangements through, 102, 107; teaching IM etiquette, 105–106; widespread use among children, 101–102

Interactive toys: help your child select useful, 21–22; increasing your child's interest in, 19–26; make sure your child wins at first, 24; play with your child and, 22–24; using tactful praise when playing with, 24–26

Interests: antisocial, 162–163; cultivation of a child's, 19–20; curbing addictive and exclusive, 13–17; increasing child's interactive toys, 20–26; interfering with friendships, 11–13; too much passion for toy or, 13. *See also* Activities

Internet: monitoring your child's access to, 107; spyware blocking/content filtering for, 103–104. *See also* Computers

Invitations. *See* Play date invitations

J

Joining other children: checklist for, 64–65; coaching your child to praise other's behavior, 61; encouraging your child to try, 61–62; finding suitable public place for, 54; help your child think of approaching, 58–59; observe children at play with your child, 56–58; privately praising your child for attempts, 63; reviewing reasons for getting turned down, 59t–60; rules of etiquette for, 51–52, 53t; teaching your child how to end participation, 62–63; teaching your child the steps for, 55–56; where and when for, 52, 54. *See also* First impressions; New activities

Jump ropes, 22

L

Listening to child: ask the teacher in addition to, 173–174; be prepared to find out later, 172–173; collecting information about teasing, 198–200; to gather information on bullying, 219–222; about their fighting, 241–244; about troublesome incident and adult's complaint, 233–235; try the direct approach to, 170–172. *See also* Communication; Parents

Little League, 35–37

Loss of friendship: catching things at the early stage, 183; help your child grieve for the, 184; schedule play dates with others to cope with, 183–184; three stages of, 182–183; two common reasons for, 181–182

Loyalty to guest: enforcing rule of, 130–131; ensuring your child practices, 134–135; relational aggression combated by, 176

M

Magic Cards, 22

Mastermind, 22

Monopoly, 22

Monopoly Junior, 22

Moving away: following divorce of parents, 185–187; helping your child adjust to, 188–192

Moving away adjustment: having child continue to value old friendships, 190–191; saying good-bye on last play date, 189; strategies to meet new friends, 191–192; talk to your child about new neighborhood, 189–190; tell friends one or two months before move, 188–189

Mr. Wiggly, 22

Myth of stealing friends, 175–176

N

Negotiation: allowing your child practice in, 23–24; of deals for electronic media use, 15–16

Neighborhood activities: ADHD and matching appropriate, 251; checklist for joining, 40–41; evaluate the adult supervision of, 37–39, 256; finding friends through, 31–41; four basic rules for first time in, 35–37; gender issues and friendships, 32; getting your child to try new, 263–266; have your child try out a, 34–35;

locating and selecting, 33–34; networking opportunities at, 44–48; safety issues of, 33–34; as source for play dates, 40. *See also* Games

Neighborhood schools: cyberbullying policies by, 219; finding friends using your, 28–30; getting information from your child's teacher, 173–174; networking opportunities at, 44–48; social advantages of, 27–28. *See also* Classmates; School vacations; Teachers

Neighborhoods: locating suitable public place for playing, 54; moving and adjusting to new, 188–192; networking with parents in new, 43–48

Networking: building social support through, 43–44; Plan A and B for talking to other moms, 46–47; steps to more effective, 45–48; times and places for, 44–45. *See also* Trading information

New activities: evaluating the, 264–266; four basic rules for first time at, 35–37; making a pact about attending, 264; picking an easy activity at first, 263–264. *See also* Joining other children

New communities: finding social support in, 43–44; meeting and networking with other parents in, 45–48; moving and child's adjustment to, 188–192; times and places to network in, 44–45

O

One-sided friendships, 160–161

Overscheduled children, 6t–7

P

Parcheesi, 22

Parent monitoring: child's cell phone and computer use, 107; during the play date, 117–118

Parents: cautiously involving yourself in activities, 39; dealing with children who bully, 217–225; discouraging poor friendship choices, 159–167; encouraging child to try new activity, 34–35; encouraging wise friendship choices, 153–158; evaluating activity adult supervision, 37–39; getting to know other child's, 118; handling adult complaints about your child, 229–238; helping your child deal with stolen friend, 178–179; helping your child through loss of friendship, 183–184; monitoring child's computer and cell phone use, 107; networking with other, 43–48; setting up play date with other child's, 112–114; stopping rumors about your child, 206–208; stopping your child's bullying, 253–257; supervising during the play date, 117–118; teaching child how to join others at play, 54–65; teaching the four basic rules for new activities, 35–37; teaching your child to make fun of teasing, 198–203; training to help children with ADHD, 251; when to step in to resolve conflict, 136–137. See also Listening to child
Patterson, G. R., 212
Penalties: for breaking the bullying rules, 256–257; for complaints by adults on inappropriate behavior, 235–236; for each instance of fighting, 244
Pinewood Derby, 67
Play date conflicts/arguments: age differences and, 133t; checklist for, 139–142; play date follow-up to avoid, 137–138; preparations to avoid, 126–131; ways to avoid play date, 137–138; when parent should step in to resolve, 136–137

Play date guests: being loyal to, 130–131, 134–135, 176; don't criticize, 129–130; four rules on how to treat, 128–130, 131–133, 134–135; the guest is always right rule, 128–129; polite ways of avoiding conflict with, 130t; preparing your child to be gracious to, 116–117, 127–131
Play date hosts: being loyal to guests, 130–131, 134–135, 176; example of poor, 125–126; four rules for being good, 128–130; parent's role in enforcing rules of, 131–133, 134–135; parent's role ensuring loyalty to guest, 135; preparing your child to be gracious, 116–117, 127–131
Play date invitations: accepting, 138–139; age limits on child making, 95–96; arranging with one child at a time, 85; be firm about not reinviting difficult child, 166–167; making the, 48; reciprocating, 119–121; strategies for postponing acceptance of, 137–138
Play dates: age limits on child arranging their own, 95–96; arranging with one child at a time, 85; be firm about not reinviting difficult child to, 166–167; checklists for, 122–123, 139–142; for children with ADHD, 252; children's roles in planning, 88t; cleaning up and preparing for, 115–116; ensuring your child likes arranged, 40; follow-up with your child after, 119; getting to know other child's parents at pick up, 118; handling stolen friends during, 175–179; having fun, 109–123; how to change boring, 129t; insisting on adult supervision during, 256; introducing idea to other parent, 47–48; making sure

siblings are busy elsewhere during, 114–115; moving away and saying good-bye on last, 189; obstacles to rewarding, 109–110; planning around day camp schedule, 148; planning, 110–112; prime times for, 5t; reciprocating, 119–121; setting up with other child's parents, 112–114; snacks during, 116; texting used to arrange, 102, 107; time needed for, 4. *See also* Activities; Friendship groups; Hosts

Playing: becoming a good sport when, 67–77; checklist for joining other children, 64–65; using tactful praise of child when, 24–26; teaching your child to join others at, 51–65; with your child, 22–24. *See also* Toys

Poor supervisor qualities, 38

Poorly behaved children, 161–162

Popular kids: avoiding friendships with, 159–160; avoiding groups of, 82

Praise/praising: for being a good sport, 74; coaching your child to give, 61; tactful, 24–26; to your child for attempts to join others, 63; to your child for wise friendship choices, 157–158

R

Ramsey, E., 212

Reciprocating play dates, 119–121

Rejection, 59t–60

Relational aggression: dealing with stolen friend form of, 176–179; example of, 175–176

Reputation: avoiding children with poor, 161–162; gathering information on child's, 156–157; helping your child overcome a negative, 268; stopping rumors that harm your child's, 206–208

Reverse cheating, 24

Rules. *See* Behavior rules

Rumors: how they get started, 205–206; stopping harm to your child's reputation by, 206–208; talking to parent of child starting the, 206–207

S

Sad behavior: patterns of, 259–260t, 262–263; trying new activities and overcoming, 263–266

Safety issues: cell phones for emergencies, 101; IM blocking, 106–107; increasing Internet use, 103–107; spyware blocking/content filtering for computers, 103–104; when selecting neighborhood activities, 33–34

School vacations: camps for children with special needs during, 146–147; day camps during, 144–145, 147–150; learning to make the most out of, 143–144; sleepover camps during, 145–146. *See also* Neighborhood schools

Shy behavior: patterns of, 259–260t; trying new activities and overcoming, 263–266

Siblings, 114–115

Siedler, Mark, 153–154, 155

Snacks (play date), 116

Social skills training, 251

Social support: divorce and maintaining friendship, 187–188; emotional category of, 44; helpful support category of, 44; networking to build, 43–44

Social world problems: allowing child time to share their, 172–173; asking teacher about possible, 173–174; challenge of finding out about, 169; direct approach to learning about, 170–172; divorce and moving away, 185–192; fighting, 211–216, 239–246; loss of close friend, 181–184; stolen friends, 175–179; teasing, 195–203. *See also* Behavioral problems; Bullying

Sportsmanship. *See* Good sportsmanship
Spyware blocking, 103–104
Stimulant medication, 250–251
Stolen friends: giving a second chance to, 179; having your child confront her, 178–179; listening to your child's account of, 178; myth of, 175–176; options for dealing with, 176–177
Structured activities: Cub Scouts, 6*t*, 8–9, 34, 67, 146, 264–265; finding friends through neighborhood, 31–41; networking opportunities at, 44–48; team sports, 33, 35–39; time spent on weekly, 4
Supervision. *See* Adult supervision; Teachers

T

Tactful praise, 24–26
Tactless feedback, 197
Teachers: checking back with complaining, 236–237, 244–245; children who challenge, 229–238; complaints about your child's fighting by, 240–245; contacting parents of children suggested by, 29–30; finding friends by contacting your child's, 28–29; informing them of bullying situation, 222–224; stopping rumors by talking to, 207–208. *See also* Adult supervision; Neighborhood schools
Team sports: cautiously involving yourself in, 39; evaluating adult supervision of, 37–39; four basic rules to follow for, 35–37; friendship benefits of neighborhood, 33
Teasing: characteristics of, 195–197; definition of, 195; humorous comebacks to, 200–203; ineffective responses to, 197–198; motivations behind, 195–197; tactless feedback versus, 197; teaching your child to make fun of, 198–203. *See also* Bullying

Technology: computer use, 3–4, 103–105, 218–219; cyberbullying using, 218–219; texting and IM (instant messaging), 101–107, 191, 218–219. *See also* Electronic media
Telephone use: checklist for trading information during, 98–99; gender differences in, 80*t*; limiting level of disclosure during, 89; making the call for play date, 94–96; practicing with your child on, 91–92; setting rules of behavior, 92–93; starting with a practice call, 93–94; teaching child how to end conversation, 97–98; teaching your child how to trade information, 88–89; teaching your child to plan play date, 89–99; as tool in developing friends, 87–89. *See also* Cell phones
Television: as addiction interfering with friendships, 11–13; average time spent per week on, 3–4; dropping time spent on, 6; negotiating deals over use of, 15–16; removing easy access to, 14; setting a reasonable weekly schedule of, 14–15
Texting: character limit, entering, and acronyms for, 102–103; cyberbullying using, 218–219; etiquette rules for, 105–106; play date arrangements through, 102, 107; widespread use among children, 101–102
Time issues: how to free up time for friends, 4–10; misplacing and giving away our time, 3–4
Tomboys, 32
Toys: icebreaker, 69; increasing interest in interactive, 19–26; too much passion for specific, 13. *See also* Playing
Trading information: checklist for, 98–99; practicing with your child, 91–92; setting rules of behavior on

telephone, 92–93; starting with a
practice call, 93–94; teaching child
how to end conversation, 97–98;
teaching how to leave answering
machine message, 89–92; two
reasons for teaching child, 88–89.
See also Networking
TV addiction, 12–13

V

Video game play: as addiction
interfering with friendships, 11–12;
average time spent per week on,
3–4; negotiating deals over use of,
15–16; removing easy access to, 14;
setting a reasonable weekly
schedule of, 14–15
Voice tone, 171, 178

W

Winning at all costs, 68t
Worried behavior: patterns of, 259–
260t, 261–262; trying new activities
and overcoming, 263–266